GREENHOUSE

GARDENER

Greenhouse Gardener

David Shelton

Galley Press

Contents

First published in Great Britain in 1979 by
Octopus Books Limited

This edition published in 1988 by
Galley Press
in association with
Octopus Books Limited
Michelin House, 81 Fulham Road
London SW3 6RB

ISBN 0 86136 047 8

Printed by Mandarin Offset in Hong Kong

1 Choosing a Greenhouse

The purpose of a greenhouse is to provide plants with a more sympathetic growing environment than would be possible in the open air. While providing plants with all the light they need, a greenhouse offers both heat and protection against wind.

The earliest ancestor of the greenhouse was the high stone or brick wall built around a cultivated area. Such walls offered not only wind protection but, by retaining heat from the sun's rays, conditions warm enough to grow relatively tender crops in the borders along south-facing walls. Even the weak spring sunshine heated the walls facing the noon sun sufficiently to protect the blossoms of fruit trees against a few degrees of night-air frost. More ambitious gardeners supplemented the sun's heat with stoves built into the walls and by extending the wall capping. Today, gardeners lucky enough to have a south-facing stone or brick wall often grow tender plants against it, and fruit growers use nets to deflect spring frosts from the blossoms.

The term 'greenhouse' originated, according to one tradition, in the method used by gardeners to keep the leaves of imported orange trees green until well into the autumn. Many wealthy English travellers brought back orange trees from the Grand Tour of Mediterranean countries. The trees, growing in barrels, would normally shed their leaves in the late summer, but gardeners discovered that they would retain their leaves for up to a couple of months longer if they were protected against the autumn frosts. As a result, in many of the grander estates in England, orangeries began to appear in the late 16th century – at first open-sided buildings with thatched roofs. Later the thatch was replaced by glass, and eventually the sides and ends of the buildings were also glazed.

The orangery was, of course, a special type of building that evolved in response to the needs of particular types

of plant (exotic shrubs as well as oranges) growing out of their normal environment. But it serves to emphasize the first decision that the gardener needs to make when he is planning to buy (or build) a greenhouse: what exactly is it to be used for? The question is especially important if you are planning to grow not one type of plant but a range of crops throughout the year. Cropping programmes can vary greatly, of course, and by the same token they demand a great variety of growing conditions.

Some crops, such as tomatoes, mid-season chrysanthemums, and vegetables, will be grown in the border soil (the soil around the base of the interior wall). Since these plants need a lot of direct sunlight to promote growth, it follows that the greenhouse must be glazed virtually to ground level on all sides. Moreover, the greenhouse must be high enough to allow the tomatoes and chrysanthemums, in particular, to attain their full growing height. In general, a greenhouse with vertical rather than sloping sides would seem preferable for tall-growing plants in the border soil. But the question is not quite as simple as that. The *angle* of slope (which can vary considerably) is an important factor. Slightly sloping sides will do little to impede growth – and they will admit more light than vertical sides. But if the angle is great, you will not be able to raise tall plants in the part of the border soil next to the greenhouse wall.

In the case of pot plants, and where an area is being set aside for plant propagation, the plants and young stock will usually be grown on benching. This will need to be of sufficient height to allow one to tend the plants without having to bend over them;

Above left Greenhouses became popular in Victorian times. **Right** A modern conservatory based on a 19th-century design.

and the light beneath the benching will be of little, if any, value. In such a case the lower sides of the greenhouse may be made of brick or board. These materials have the advantage of allowing less heat to escape than does glass.

As I will be explaining later, heat conservation is an important factor in greenhouse gardening, and if the greenhouse is to be used both for growing crops in the border and on benching it is not unusual to have a solid 1 m (3 ft) high side wall on one side and glazing to the ground on the other side. On the face of it this is an attractive solution, but in practice it prevents any simple system of crop rotation.

To make a final choice the prospective owner will have to take his considerations a stage further. Is the site an exposed one? Do the crops to be grown need fairly high temperatures? If the

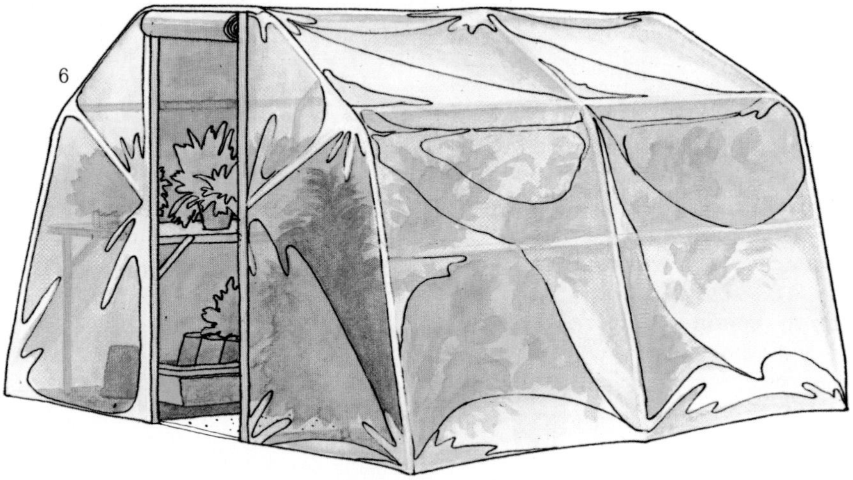

Above Drawings show typical forms and materials of modern greenhouses: 1 Straight-sided alloy-framed; 2 Sloping-sided alloy-framed; 3 Alloy-framed lean-to; 4 Polygonal alloy-framed; 5 Partly boarded cedar-framed; 6 Polythene-covered steel-framed. **Far left** Permanent benching needs to be sturdily constructed to take the considerable weight of a pot-plant display. **Near left** Cucumbers (cordon-trained) growing in raised beds of well-rotted compost. The partly boarded sides of the greenhouse reduce heat loss.

answers to such questions are 'yes', then the advantages of one solid wall might well outweigh the advantages of being able to alternate the border in which the crops are being grown.

The choice of a greenhouse does not rest simply between those with glass to the ground and those with side walls made partly of some solid material. Perhaps a simpler and cheaper structure will suffice, in which case it is necessary to consider the materials other than glass that can be used.

Gardeners today realize that the best results are obtained by providing optimum growing conditions for their plants, and this usually means protecting them from the extremes of the elements. Consider for a moment what is meant by 'optimum conditions'. In the shoot zone – that part of a plant above the level of the soil – light, warmth, and moisture have to be available in balanced proportions, and we now know that the level of carbon dioxide (CO_2) in the air is also critical. In the root zone the growing medium has to furnish the plant with nutrients and moisture in addition to providing an anchorage. In later chapters I will be giving some guidance about how to obtain the optimum conditions for some major crops.

Light

Light is one of the most important factors in growth, and consequently designers of greenhouses aim to let in as much as possible. In theory the hemispherical shape is best, for the sun's rays are always at 90° to the panes facing towards it, and consequently less light is deflected, especially if the glass is clean (a point often forgotten by greenhouse owners, too few of whom clean their glass on a regular basis).

If the hemisphere is the ideal shape, why are all greenhouses not so built? The answer is that it would be impractical. For instance, it is difficult to fit doors into a curving surface, and the materials the designer has at his disposal – glass, timber, steel, and light alloy – are most readily and cheaply available in straight forms. The same difficulties arise with ventilators, which need to be incorporated into the structure, and with benching and shelving, which would have to follow the curve of the hemispherical wall. Yet another problem is how to make the best use of the growing area. Tending the plants and spacing them correctly is much more difficult in hemispherical greenhouses than in rectangular ones. For these reasons the conventional greenhouse shapes continue to predominate, although there are plenty of interesting variations on the basic themes.

The slender frames of alloy greenhouses allow the maximum amount of light to reach the plants. In this example, however, faulty siting – near a large tree and with the back wall against a fence – considerably reduces the amount of direct sunlight reaching the greenhouse interior throughout the day.

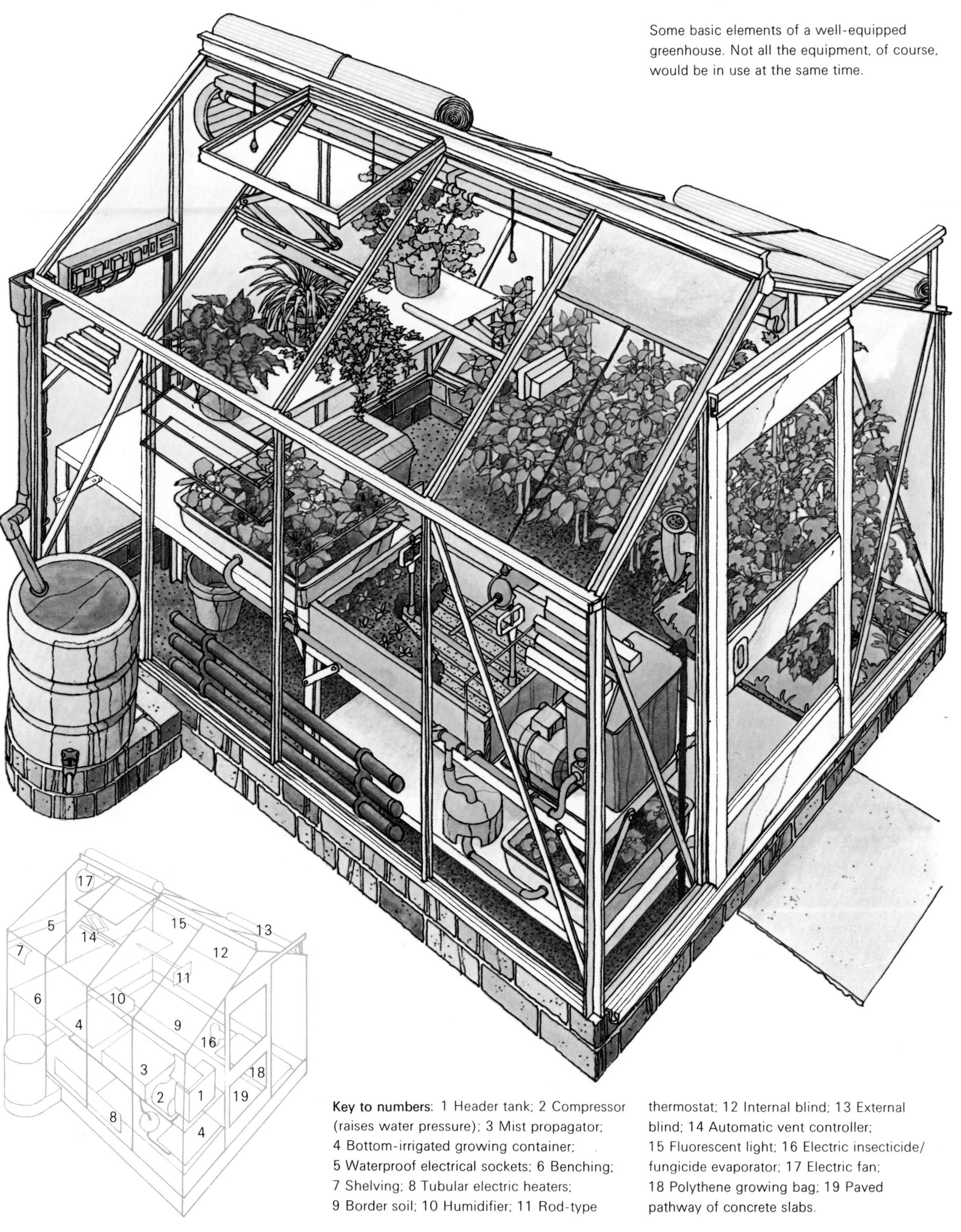

Some basic elements of a well-equipped greenhouse. Not all the equipment, of course, would be in use at the same time.

Key to numbers: 1 Header tank; 2 Compressor (raises water pressure); 3 Mist propagator; 4 Bottom-irrigated growing container; 5 Waterproof electrical sockets; 6 Benching; 7 Shelving; 8 Tubular electric heaters; 9 Border soil; 10 Humidifier; 11 Rod-type thermostat; 12 Internal blind; 13 External blind; 14 Automatic vent controller; 15 Fluorescent light; 16 Electric insecticide/ fungicide evaporator; 17 Electric fan; 18 Polythene growing bag; 19 Paved pathway of concrete slabs.

Heat and ventilation

Given adequate light, one of the most important attributes of a greenhouse is the way it deals with the potentially conflicting needs of heat retention and ventilation. Greenhouse designers have devoted much thought to the problem of retaining heat. Some years ago double glazing seemed likely to be the answer. In practice, however, the method has serious disadvantages: the two layers of transparent material cut out a great deal of light; the sun's rays take much longer to heat the greenhouse; and the space between the transparent layers attract algae. Moreover, double glazing is considerably more expensive than single glazing.

Whatever the shape or design of the greenhouse, adequate ventilation must be provided. Greenhouses used to have relatively few ventilators and those that were fitted were often small. As a consequence, on sunny days the greenhouse got too hot for the plants to grow happily, and gardeners were forced to provide shade to prevent damage. For the modern designer the problem is to provide adequate ventilation while avoiding draughts. As a rule the ventilator area should be equal to at least one fifth of the total interior floor area. If ventilators need to be covered

Good ventilation is essential to the healthy growth of greenhouse plants.

by lightweight netting to keep out birds, the ventilator area should be increased, for such nets substantially decrease the effect of the vents. For simplicity of manufacture ventilators are usually confined to the roof area; on the more expensive designs, both roof and side ventilators may be available, and these are preferable because they allow greater control to be exercised over the growing environment. Doors should not be used as ventilators unless the doorways are fitted with blinds; otherwise the draughts that inevitably develop are likely to damage the plants near the doors. Incidentally, sliding doors are generally preferable to hinged ones because the opening can be regulated more easily.

Structural materials

Aluminium alloys are now widely used for the framework of greenhouses, and the latest extrusion techniques enable refinements such as drip channels and ventilator hinges to be neatly built in. Alloys of this type need virtually no maintenance, and because of their great strength the glazing bars can be of narrow section, so that they throw little shadow. When new the alloys are usually bright metal, but oxides of aluminium tend to form on the surface over a period of time; although, unlike rust on steel, these oxides do not weaken the alloy, they cause its surface to turn dull. Some manufacturers enamel the alloy to prevent this happening, and if appearance is a major consideration the extra cost of this treatment may seem worthwhile.

Steel is now less widely used for greenhouse structures than hitherto but is nevertheless finding favour with some manufacturers of polythene-clad greenhouses, for it has great strength and yet can be easily bent into hoops with the simplest of equipment. Steel will rust rapidly in the greenhouse environment unless it is treated in some way. Galvanizing gives long-lasting protection. However, care is necessary in the transport and erection of treated steelwork to ensure that the galvanizing is not removed. Touching up suspect places with a special paint will protect the surface against rusting.

Gardeners who favour wooden greenhouses are usually quick to point out that heat losses from aluminium alloys are greater than from wood, and that aluminium greenhouses consequently become colder more quickly as temperatures fall. This is so, but in my estimation the advantages of the narrow section of the alloy glazing bars outweigh those of the heavier-sectioned timber-framed greenhouse.

Until a few years ago wood was used extensively by greenhouse builders and the many wooden greenhouses still in use demonstrate that wood has a long life provided it is properly cared for. It is the necessity for regular painting or other treatment both inside and out that has persuaded many gardeners to turn to the alloy-framed greenhouse, but wood is still preferred by the more traditionally-minded, not least for its appearance.

Softwood, mainly pine, is the favourite wood for glazing bars, while hardwoods are normally used for the sills. Modern techniques of preserving wood are now widely employed, but prospective purchasers should ensure that such treatments have been properly carried out, ideally under pressure, to force the preservative into all the timber. Simply brushing on such preservative is virtually useless.

Some manufacturers use a hardwood such as oak throughout, and greenhouses of this type have a long, relatively maintenance-free life. Western red cedar is an attractive looking wood and has been used in the more expensive greenhouse ranges for many years. It is not as strong as some other woods, so the timber sections need to be somewhat thicker, but its attractions are the colour, which looks well in almost every garden setting, and freedom from the need for painting. In fact, no paint is applied at all, just a suitable preserving oil which needs to be brushed on every two or three years.

Many gardeners of the older generation still prefer wood-framed greenhouses, for they consider that they provide a better growing climate for their plants. There appears to be no scientific evidence for this, but if you are prepared to spend more time on maintaining a wooden-framed greenhouse you will certainly not be at a disadvantage, as far as plant cultivation is concerned, compared to those working in alloy structures.

Glass

Glass used in horticulture is usually 3 mm thick (24 oz/sq ft) and the standard quality available is generally good. Nevertheless, when buying a greenhouse it is as well to enquire what weight, or thickness, of glass is supplied; whether it is of British manufacture or imported; whether it is supplied directly by the retailer or comes from a glass distributor; and what arrangements there are for replacing panes of glass that might get broken in transit. It is a sensible precaution to examine a sample pane, for the quality may vary considerably, and glass that gives distorted images may be unsuitable in some situations. Generally speaking, the larger the panes of glass the better, for they will allow greater light admission.

A bed has to be provided between the glass and the frame, and while linseed-oil putty may still be used in wooden-framed greenhouses, alternatives are available that are in some respects superior. The main drawback with conventional putty is that, unless the exposed edges are sealed with paint, it dries out after a while. Eventually cracks will form, letting in water and perhaps causing drips. There are now 'never-set' putties, most of which are easily applied from the nozzle of a simple purpose-made applicator. Another method which is now widely used consists of ribbons of adhesive-coated plastic, which are wound from a drum straight on to the glazing bars. The ribbon is claimed to retain its adhesive properties for many years – an important advantage when it comes to replacing a broken pane.

Alloy-framed greenhouses are generally provided with simple clips to hold the glass panes in place. Make sure these are of a non-rusting type, and consider how difficult it would be to replace a broken pane. Sooner or later this will be necessary, and the speed with which it can be done varies enormously with different types of fastening. Panes of glass will usually overlap, and should do so by about 12 mm ($\frac{1}{2}$ in). The overlap should not be too great, because algae will inevitably grow there, cutting out the light; on the other hand, too small an overlap allows rain to enter and creates unwanted draughts. On the sides of the greenhouse the glass panes may butt together, and there is nothing against this providing they fit snugly, edge to edge.

At this point you should be able to decide what kind of greenhouse you need. You will be able to decide, for instance, what structural material (alloy, steel, or wood) you prefer; the need or otherwise to provide for benching; and the type and extent of glazing and ventilation.

Costs

Obviously, the cost of a greenhouse depends primarily upon its size. The simplest method of comparing the costs of different makes is to divide the price of each by its floor area, which will give you the cost per square foot or metre. But other factors will determine whether you are getting the best value for your money.

Your calculations as to the size of greenhouse required should be based on the types of plants you intend to grow, the amount of time you can spare for this work, the space available in your garden, and, of course, the amount of money you are prepared to spend. When calculating the floor area needed, bear in mind that the nett area can be increased if the greenhouse has provision for shelves to be fitted, but that the area will be decreased by the amount of space you will have to allow for pathways, internal supports, and other obstructions. In this connection, bear in mind that long, narrow greenhouses need a relatively higher proportion of floor area devoted to paths, while circular or polygonal greenhouses may present difficulties in the spacing and tending of crops.

The basic advertised price of a greenhouse does not necessarily tell the whole story about costs: there are often 'hidden' extras. The most important of these concerns the foundations. Many manufacturers offer a base for their greenhouses, but it usually costs extra. In some cases a concrete or brick base will need to be constructed and the cost of this, too, must be calculated. It is important to build foundations at least to the minimum specification recommended by the greenhouse manufacturer. Neglect to do this may later result in a large number of broken panes of glass or, at worst, the possibility of the greenhouse shifting in strong winds.

The cost of extras should also be calculated and the different types compared for quality and design. Some manufacturers offer greenhouse benching which is free standing and easily erected and dismantled. Others offer staging of a more robust design fixed to the greenhouse itself and intended to be more or less permanent. Neither alternative is better than the other: your choice will depend on the use to which you intend to put your greenhouse, although removable benching is obviously an advantage if you are contemplating mixed cropping programmes using benching and borders.

I have already mentioned the use of shelving, and this can be invaluable in springtime when most greenhouses are bulging with young plants. However it is unwise to fit shelving either to the side wall or suspended from the glazing bars unless this is recommended by the greenhouse manufacturer; otherwise the weight of a shelf-full of plants in pots and boxes, which can be considerable, may distort the frame. The best shelving is both robust and light in weight but is also rather expensive.

Established plants make a fine display in this lean-to conservatory.

Last, but not least, it is important to know how easily the greenhouse can be erected, as help with erection may be charged for. Greenhouses of aluminium alloy usually bolt together in a straightforward manner, and most gardeners will have little difficulty assembling them. Greenhouses of wood are likely to have heavier sections and assembly may be more complicated, especially when it comes to fitting doors and ventilators. The system of glazing will possibly determine whether erecting the greenhouse is within the capacity of the gardener or whether a specialist builder will need to be employed.

Finally, consider likely maintenance costs over periods of, say, five and ten years. With alloy-framed structures erected according to the manufacturer's directions, maintenance should be negligible. With wooden greenhouses of softwood it would be wise to calculate on repainting the exterior every four to five years and the interior every five to six years. In the case of greenhouses built of western red cedar, allow for treatment every two to three years.

Lean-tos and frames

Lean-to greenhouses and conservatories are alternatives worth considering for some situations. In most respects the same factors need to be taken into account as when choosing a conventional greenhouse. As most lean-to structures nowadays are built on to the home a word of warning is necessary: a greenhouse full of plants cuts out a lot of light, and if it covers a window the room will be noticeably darker. On the other hand the provision of services such as electricity and water is made much simpler.

Lean-to growing cases, tended from the outside, are an alternative where space is limited or where something less expensive is required. Growing cases may provide the opportunity for flat dwellers with suitable balconies to join the ranks of greenhouse owners. The framework is usually made of aluminium alloy and growing cases are supplied complete with shelves, thereby allowing a sizeable cropping area in a comparatively small space.

Designers of garden frames have improved upon the basic frame to such

Above A garden frame in course of erection. The interior will be painted white to provide better light reflection. Timber is best preserved using pressure treatments. **Left** This conservatory was tailor made to blend in with its surroundings. Wooden structures, if regularly painted, have a long, useful life.

an extent that gardeners may confidently grow in them plants they would at one time have cultivated solely in a greenhouse, Height is perhaps the main factor limiting the range of plants that can be grown in frames. Most greenhouse owners regard a frame as an important adjunct to the greenhouse, moving into it plants requiring some hardening off before they are planted out in the garden.

Plastic-covered greenhouses

Undoubtedly the biggest rival nowadays to the conventional greenhouse is the polythene-covered structure, of which several designs are available. Its popularity is due to its relative cheapness, resulting from the simplicity of the framework and the sold-in-a-carton approach. The basic framework in most cases is of tubular alloy or galvanized steel, and 600-gauge polythene sheeting is the usual covering material. Several factors affect the life of the sheeting so it is not easy to be definite as to how often it will need replacing.

Polythene life will be extended by the addition of an ultra-violet inhibitor (UVI) during the manufacturing process, and polythene so treated is now widely available. The tautness of the cover and the care with which it is put over its frame can make all the difference between a long and a short life. It is advisable first to wrap tape round those parts of the frame which might snag the cover and to put on the polythene sheet on a warm day. Polythene expands considerably when warm, and it is possible to get it drum tight by following the manufacturer's recommendations in this respect. Some greenhouses are supplied with polythene sheeting tailored to fit like a glove. As a result there are no unsightly folds in the cover and the effect is much neater. However, in the manufacturing process this requires welding the polythene, which is likely to deteriorate more quickly at the welds. With a measure of luck the polythene should need replacing only every two years,

Left above A lean-to greenhouse with roof and side ventilators. Narrow-section glazing bars cut out the minimum of light.
Left below A lean-to growing case.

although in very exposed situations annual re-covering may be necessary.

Greenhouses of this sort provide growing conditions different from the conventional glasshouse and have to be used differently, particularly as regards watering and ventilation. Nevertheless, almost all plants thrive in them and the gardening scene is likely to see many more greenhouses of this type in the future.

RIGID PLASTIC GLAZING The 'cheap-and-nasty' image of rigid plastic is still firmly entrenched in the minds of many gardeners; but it is certainly worth considering carefully what advantages – not least in cost – rigid-plastic-covered structures offer before making a final choice. Of the plastics available, extruded acrylic sheet 0.25 mm (0.01 in) thick is strong and flexible and has a life of 10 to 20 years when used in greenhouses. Clear PVC is available in corrugated form to provide the necessary strength, and a 10-year life can be expected for this. These plastics are satisfactory alternatives to glass, and while they are considerably more expensive, the framework to which they are fixed can be simplified, so that overall costs may differ only slightly.

For the newcomer to greenhouse gardening the apparently bewildering choice of structures can be narrowed down by following the steps I have suggested in this chapter. It may seem at first sight to be rather a laborious process, but in the final outcome it will save you time, frustration – and possibly a great deal of expense.

A polythene-covered greenhouse. To compare costs with conventional greenhouses, first calculate the area that can be cropped.

Siting

Many gardeners have little choice as to where to site their greenhouse. Letting in the maximum amount of light must be the overriding factor of the many that need to be considered, and the orientation of the greenhouse will have a bearing on this. Whether the ridge of the greenhouse is best run on a north-south or an east-west axis will depend to a great extent on the nature of the cropping programme. If cultivation of winter and early spring crops is important, then the east-west axis will provide better interior light conditions in winter than any other. This is because the hours of winter daylight are relatively few and adequate sunlight is available only between about 10 am and 4 pm. With the side of the greenhouse facing the available sun there will be less shadow from the framework of the structure and maximum penetration of the sun's rays through the transparent covering. A similar greenhouse on a north-south axis would have its end facing the sun at mid-day and sunlight into the house would be broken up by many shadows.

On the other hand, if the cropping emphasis is on summer and autumn crops the north-south axis is to be preferred. In mid-summer the side of the greenhouse faces the early morning sun and consequently it warms up quickly. At mid-day, when the sun is high in the sky and outdoor temperatures are soaring, the end of the greenhouse faces the sun and the shading effect may prove beneficial. As the sun sets in the west, its rays again fall on the side of the greenhouse, keeping up temperatures well into the evening.

Avoid any shading of the site by overhanging branches, tall fences, or nearby shrubs. Overhanging branches can be particularly troublesome, for the drips from them dirty the greenhouse quickly and in gales quite small twigs banging against the greenhouse are capable of breaking glass. Even shrubs 2 m (6 ft) in height will throw long shadows in winter-time, and it may be necessary to rearrange some of the plants near the greenhouse in order not to deprive it of light.

Winter: north-south axis brings shadow from frames.

Summer: north-south axis best for summer/autumn crops.

Winter: east-west axis best for winter/early spring crops.

Summer: east-west axis may cause mid-day overheating.

Greenhouse sites to avoid: beneath a large tree, beside tall-growing shrubs, against a north-facing wall, and in a position exposed to winds.

The condition of the area of soil that will be used as borders is also important. Soil that tends to become waterlogged in winter is unlikely to dry out simply because it is covered by a greenhouse: water has a great capacity for moving sideways in many soils. If plants are to be grown in the borders of a greenhouse on such a site, it will be necessary to raise the soil level 150 to 200 mm (6 to 8 in), preferably before erecting the greenhouse. Ensure the soil added is topsoil rather than subsoil, and take the opportunity to enrich it by adding peat or well-rotted garden compost.

Once the site has been chosen the conventional greenhouse is likely to remain there for many years and provide an important garden feature. This often leads to problems if crops are grown in borders because soil pests and diseases can build up over the years, and a falling-off in the general health of successive crops is inevitable unless some form of soil renewal or sterilization is practised. On the other hand, the lightweight plastic greenhouse, the polythene-covered greenhouse, and growing cases and frames can be moved to a fresh site with ease. If you can do this every two years, you are unlikely to be worried by soil-sickness problems.

The site must be flat and as nearly horizontal as possible. There are several reasons for this, quite apart from the need to make the structure stable. For instance, hot air rises, and greenhouses longer than about 5 m (16 ft) that run up a steepish slope will have a temperature differential of several degrees from one end to the other. Another more obvious problem arises with watering, for the lower parts of the borders in a sloping greenhouse will always be wetter than the higher parts. Finally, a sloping site makes staging difficult to erect and keep firm, and the plants growing on shelves and benching are more difficult to manage.

Be careful how you set about levelling a site: the top 200 mm (8 in) of soil should first be removed and set to one side, and the underlying subsoil levelled; the topsoil is then replaced. This is quite a laborious job if the greenhouse has a large floor area. An alternative method is to construct a base of bricks or concrete blocks in such a manner as to take up variations in soil level. Some makes of polythene-covered greenhouse are designed to allow erection on gently sloping sites without any need for moving soil. Such greenhouses have foundation tubes which are driven into the soil, any uneveness of the ground being taken up by varying the depth to which the tubes are sunk.

The greenhouse is often a prominent feature in the garden and children at play, especially with ball games, are likely to be the main cause of glass breakages. If protection becomes necessary, 25 mm (1 in) wire netting erected on a simple framework 1 m (3 ft) from the greenhouse is effective and cuts out the minimum of light. The alternative may be to tuck away the structure out of sight, but vandalism and theft of produce may be the price you pay for doing so.

On exposed sites protection from the wind is important, particularly winds from the north and east. Glasshouses are not airtight, for air moves between the panes of glass as well as through closed ventilators and doors. Even in still conditions one to two air changes an hour can be expected, and more air changes will occur as wind speed rises over the glass area. The ideal screen is a filter rather than a windbreak and is about 60 per cent solid; hedges and shrubs are good for this purpose. An alternative is fine wire netting – a double fence of netting some 75 to 150 mm (3 to 6 in) apart provides the almost perfect filter, while cutting out little light. A fence of this sort may be well worth constructing if the greenhouse is being heated and keeping the temperature up, or at least regular, is important.

Vallota, fuchsias, and pelargoniums provide colour at different levels in this greenhouse constructed of western red cedar.

Erecting an alloy greenhouse

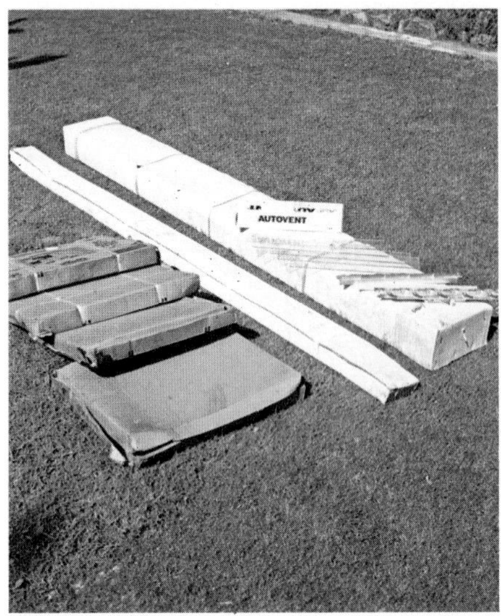

1

Many greenhouses are now supplied in pack form. Be careful to check that all the listed components, screws, nuts, bolts, and so on are present before you begin erection.

2

The site needs to be raked level to provide a solid support for the base. Keep the greenhouse as far away as possible from any solid fences that would cast a shadow on it.

3

Ensure that the base is firmly secured to the foundation, otherwise the greenhouse may shift in high winds – a common cause of glass breakage.

7

Although alloy frames are light in weight, you may need another pair of hands at this stage in order to prevent the sections from flexing.

8

Take care to follow the manufacturer's step-by-step instructions exactly – the sequence of assembly is likely to vary from make to make.

9

Precision built in the factory, the correctly installed ventilators when closed should make a snug, draught-proof fit into the framework.

4
Assemble the sections of the frame on level ground nearby. Avoid getting particles of soi on the glazing bars; if necessary, lay down some plastic sheeting to work on.

5
Most householders will possess the few tools required for assembly. Double check that all screws and nuts and bolts are tight.

6
The principal sections of the frame assembled and ready for erection on the base.

10
Preparation for glazing: carefully dust down all the glazing bars before placing the mastic glazing strips into position.

11
In this greenhouse model the vertical panes of glass overlap. Spring clips hold the glass firmly but they allow broken panes to be changed easily and quickly.

12
Work completed. Although the structure looks complicated, erection of such greenhouses is well within the compass of most amateur gardeners.

2 Services and Equipment

Water

Greenhouse plants need a considerable amount of water, especially on hot, sunny days, and it is essential to ensure that the water, from whatever source, is not contaminated in any way. As a rough guide to quantities required, a single sturdy tomato plant carrying several trusses of fruit will require at least 1.5 l ($2\frac{1}{2}$ pints) of water per day applied to the root zone, in addition to that required for spraying over the foliage and damping down the greenhouse.

RAINWATER If the greenhouse has been fitted with gutters it is a good idea to lead the rainwater into a water butt or tank, for rainwater is soft and suitable for all plants. In the larger greenhouse, the tank can be situated within the structure, either above ground or sunk into the soil. The water will thus be warmed to some extent; and although there is no scientific evidence to show that warmed water is better than cold, many gardeners prefer to use it.

MAINS SUPPLY If a permanent mains-water supply is taken to the greenhouse it will have to comply with the local water-authority regulations; this may mean that you have to run the supply pipe in a trench 750 mm to 1 m (30 to 36 in) deep. A semi-rigid plastic piping simplifies this task, and if compression fittings are used this brings the job into the realm of the handyman. A mains supply is essential if you wish to install a mist propagation unit or a drip system of irrigation, and you will also have to include a fine filter in the coupling line. Where pot plants are a major part of the cropping programme, installation of a permanent sub-irrigated bench allows the plants to take up just the amount of water they require when they need it. Systems of this type also require connecting to the mains.

Incidentally, it will be a good idea to enquire (if you do not already know) whether your mains water is hard or soft. Very hard (that is, alkaline) water should not be applied to acid-loving plants, such as azaleas. The more ambitious gardener may wish to install a water-softening system. A cheaper alternative is to use stored rainwater.

Electricity

For many greenhouse owners a supply of electricity will be essential to make the best use of their investment. It will be needed for interior lighting, so that greenhouse work can be done in the evening after work during the short days of winter and spring. Ordinary incandescent lights will be suitable for this. Electricity may also be needed for heating a propagating frame, and local heating of this type can be the most economical way of propagating plants. Electric soil-warming units are becoming popular as a reasonably inexpensive method of boosting the growth of plants in greenhouse borders. Electricity may also be required for general heating, for providing supplementary fan ventilation, for activating mist-propagators, and for supplementary lighting of some crops.

Electricity can be particularly dangerous in the greenhouse because there is normally a considerable amount of moisture about. For example, during damping down the humidity of the greenhouse interior is raised by spraying overall with a fine spray of water. For this reason it is essential to use special waterproof fittings both in the installation of the mains supply and on each piece of equipment. A system installed by a qualified electrician will ensure that sufficient safety measures are taken, and it remains only for you to make sure that your electrical equipment is properly earthed and fitted with the fuses recommended by the manufacturer. The electricity supply to the greenhouse can be above or below ground; an electrical contractor is best able to advise on this.

Gas

Gas is rarely used by the amateur gardener, but if the greenhouse is to be heated gas may well be cheaper overall than the alternatives of electricity or fuel oil. The installation of a mains gas supply is not a job for the home handyman; similarly, a supply of bottled propane for heating would need to be professionally installed.

Greenhouse interior. Rod-type thermostats (on roof frame) are widely used to control the output of electrical heating systems.

Benching

Benching or staging comes in many different types and the use to which it is to be put should determine the choice. It may be either permanent or temporary. Permanent benching will be required for pot plants, for plant-propagating units, and where you need to set aside an area as a potting bench. Semi-permanent or temporary benching will be needed where it is intended to bench up only part of the greenhouse for part of the year and to grow crops in the remaining borders. If you require benching in the spring and early summer, benching can be erected in January and removed later.

The benching framework can be of steel, aluminium alloy, or pressure-treated timber. Its strength will depend on whether the benching is to have a solid or open top surface and also on the weight it has to carry. Manufacturers of solid benching often use flat or corrugated asbestos sheeting on top of the framework, and this will allow a layer of sand or shingle to be added if required. A permanent display of pot plants would normally be staged in this manner. Open benching, commonly of welded mesh, slats of treated wood, or alloy, is valuable because it allows air to circulate more easily around the plants.

When installing benching make sure that it is the best height for you to work at comfortably. If you find it to be a bit on the low side, putting a brick beneath each leg will not only raise it but give it added stability. Do not rest the legs directly on border soil.

Bench depth is important. In the case of solid benches there should be a gap of 150 mm (6 in) between the back of the bench and the glass to enable air to flow freely around the greenhouse, and the front of the bench should be level with the edge of the centre path. Benches deeper than about 1.25 m (4 ft) will make for difficulties in tend-

Left above Sub-irrigation of pot plants is now widely practised, and there is a variety of automatic-watering systems to choose from.
Left below Temporary benching of this type is quickly erected and dismantled. The legs need to stand firmly on bricks or concrete, not directly on the soil.

ing plants at the back of the bench. If the benching is to be temporary, the ease with which it can be assembled, dismantled, and stored should be taken into consideration.

Shelving

In March, April, and May greenhouse space is at a premium, for many plants need temporary accommodation. They include bedding plants being raised from seed for summer display in open ground, vegetable plants being raised for planting out as soon as the risk of frost has passed, and the propagation of chrysanthemums, dahlias, and pelargoniums.

The erection of temporary shelving can help in this difficult period as long as the greenhouse structure is designed to take what may amount to a considerable extra weight. If in doubt consult the manufacturer or supplier before proceeding. Shelving needs to be strong and yet light in weight, and slatted alloy is often preferred to wood. The shelves may be suspended from the upper glazing bars or fixed to the side walls, but in the latter situation they may unduly shade plants on the benching. The erection of shelving must be looked upon as a temporary expedient, for if it is in position for a long period the plants growing beneath it will inevitably suffer from a reduction in the amount of light they receive. Painting shelving white helps in this respect.

Heating equipment

A greenhouse affords plants protection from the elements, and for this reason they usually grow better than they would out of doors in the same location. Unheated glasshouses provide a little protection from frost (of the order of 2 to 3°C), but unheated polythene

Right above Temporary slatted shelving should not be used, as here, for storing pots or other equipment. When not required it should be dismantled to admit more light.
Right below Permanent shelving provides useful extra space, but it limits use of the benching below it.

greenhouses under a clear sky give no protection at all.

Unheated greenhouses consequently have their effective cropping use limited to the warmer months of the year. In the south of England an eight-month period of use is possible – from March to November – but in the north the period is somewhat shorter. This is not to say that winter cropping is impossible, but the range is strictly limited and a high percentage of plants may succumb to disease. Some greenhouse heating is therefore well worthwhile. Heating the whole greenhouse can be expensive; alternatives are to divide the greenhouse into different compartments with permanent glass divisions, or to erect a temporary screen of a double layer of polythene. Yet another way of saving money is to localize the heating – warming only a propagating frame, for instance, or soil-warming a border or greenhouse bench.

Before buying heating equipment it is as well to think carefully about the minimum temperature that is to be aimed for. It is natural to think that if frost can be kept out by maintaining temperatures above 1 to 2°C semi-hardy plants will overwinter safely. In practice this is not so, for the relatively humid conditions under glass that so often accompany low outdoor temperatures create conditions in which plant diseases become rampant. There are three basic heating regimes in the greenhouse (*see* Chapter 5). Possibly most suitable for the majority of amateur growers, and giving considerable scope, is a minimum temperature of 7°C (45°F) overall, with higher local temperatures for plant propagation. Safe overwintering of a wide range of plants is possible, and many house and decorative plants will grow satisfactorily provided you exercise some care over watering and ventilation. Increasing the overall minimum temperature to 12°C (54°F) raises the heating bill considerably; and maintaining it at 18°C (65°F) would put heating costs out of the reach of most amateur gardeners.

EXPENSE As fuel prices have soared horticulturists have adapted their growing techniques. Specialist plant propagators are now offering a wide range of young rooted plants raised in high temperatures but ready for growing on in lower-temperature regimes, and this is one way in which the amateur can save on heating bills. The fitting of thin polythene of 150-gauge part way up the sides of the greenhouse for a few weeks in the spring will provide worthwhile additional protection for plants. But, as in the home, attention should first be paid to eliminating draughts, and the fitting of doors and ventilators should be checked as well as the join between the greenhouse and its foundations.

Heating costs vary enormously, depending, for example, on the region in which one lives, whether the greenhouse is in an exposed or protected situation, its height above sea level, whether it is covered with glass or polythene, the age of the structure, and so on. The following will serve as a rough guide, however.

GLASSHOUSE HEATING BY ELECTRICITY

Approximate number of units consumed per week in maintaining a minimum temperature of 7°C (45°F) during the winter months:

Floor area of greenhouse	Mild areas of England and Wales	Remainder of England and Wales	Scotland
2.5 × 1.8 m (8 × 6 ft)	30	54	60
3.7 × 2.5 m (12 × 8 ft)	45	81	90
5 × 2.5 m (16 × 8 ft)	60	105	120
6 × 3 m (20 × 10 ft)	72	126	144

Unit consumption will approximately double if a minimum temperature of 10°C (51°F) is required and will treble if 15°C (60°F) is required. Equipment suppliers or your local electricity board will usually be able to provide fairly accurate running costs for a particular district and type of greenhouse, and the board will also advise on the most suitable tariff. Because it can be thermostatically controlled, electric-heating running costs compare favourably with those of paraffin heaters if high minimum temperatures are not required.

SYSTEMS Having made the decision to instal a heating system, you then have to decide on the type. First, consider whether an existing system can be used. In the case of lean-to structures and conservatories, you may be able to extend the home central-heating system without great expense, although the heating demands differ – the home requires much of its heat during the day, whereas the greenhouse needs much of its heat at night. Those with a heated swimming pool may be able to adapt its heating equipment to serve the two purposes, pool and greenhouse heating.

Choice of fuel is wide: oil, town gas, propane, electricity, coal, anthracite, wood – even straw. Each has its advantages and disadvantages.

The commonest system is a small heater fuelled by paraffin, gas, or electricity. For the bigger greenhouse a boiler fired by oil, gas, or solid fuel from which 50 mm (2 in) hot-water pipes are run will usually provide the most economical source of heat, taking both fuel and labour costs into consideration. In such systems the heat source can be situated at ground level outside the structure, and the smoke stack should be placed so that the prevailing winds take the products of combustion away from the glass and not over it.

Paraffin heaters have a wide appeal and many good designs are available. Some have built-in water troughs to increase greenhouse humidity, but such refinements are not essential, and to my mind easy servicing is more important to ensure that the heater burns cleanly at all times, because the fumes are vented into the greenhouse. It is essential to use a high grade of paraffin;

A paraffin heater provides one of the cheapest sources of artificial heat.

inferior grades may give off sulphur, which can damage the plants.

Gas heaters using natural or bottled gas are available and while initial costs of equipment are somewhat higher than that for paraffin or electric heaters of similar output, running costs may work out cheaper.

Gas-fueled heaters can be run from bottled gas, as in this example, or from town gas.

The simplicity of electric heating has wide appeal in spite of the high cost per unit compared with other fuels. Tubular heaters were a favoured form of heating for many years, but nowadays the horticultural fan heater appears to have gained in popularity. Fan heaters distribute their heat well around the greenhouse and the gentle air movement through the plant foliage is beneficial. Both tubular and fan heaters can be thermostatically controlled, and some equipment has built-in thermostats.

Off-peak electricity is somewhat cheaper and some greenhouse gardeners have a night-storage heater installed along the central path. This type of heater requires the laying of a solid concrete path several millimetres thick through which electric warming wires are run. The depth of concrete and the number of wires required have to be calculated for each situation; your local electricity board will be able to advise you on this.

THERMOSTATS Accurate thermostatic control of heating equipment is in the interests both of economy and of the plants. Rod thermostats are commonly used, as are room thermostats of the type used in the home. Inexpensive thermostats of this kind may not give very accurate temperature control and a more expensive temperature controller might well prove cheaper in the long run. Aspirated screens protect the thermostat from radiation and at the same time provide a steady movement of air over it. Whatever type of thermostat is installed it is advisable to check it from time to time, for a faulty thermostat can quickly run up an enormous heating bill. A maximum/minimum thermometer housed in a well-vented box within the greenhouse is a worthwhile investment that will allow you to make spot checks on the thermostat. If it is faulty, have it repaired immediately.

Ventilation

Greenhouses need to be ventilated to prevent temperatures rising above those best suited to the plants being grown; high temperatures lead to stress within the plants and may cause wilting. Ventilation is also required to control humidity levels within the greenhouse. Tomatoes, for example, require a humid atmosphere at least once a day for an hour or two to allow the flowers to set, but for the remainder of the time they like a drier atmosphere.

Setting the ventilation by hand involves guessing the weather conditions for the next few hours. If a person is out at work all day, he may have to open the vents early in the morning and close them late at night. In such a case the greenhouse may suffer from very wide temperature variations, to the detriment of the plants. For these reasons money spent on automatic ventilation equipment is a good investment. Several makes of automatic vent gear are available that work on the principle of a special liquid expanding as it warms up and in so doing pushing a piston which in turn opens the ventilator. The temperature at which the vent opens and closes can be adjusted. If possible, arrange the system so that the ventilators open only on the side away from the prevailing wind.

On polythene-covered greenhouses, ventilators of the traditional type cannot be fitted; instead, a form of blind

A turbo-flow fan heater. The fan also helps to move air within the greenhouse in summer.

Soil-warming wires provide bottom heat for this bench. Note soil thermometer.

Automatic-ventilation systems help to keep the greenhouse at the required temperature.

is used in the doorway. If additional ventilation is needed, an extractor fan, thermostatically controlled, may be used, or alternatively an electric blower-heater can be rigged up to serve the same purpose.

Blinds

Plants differ as to the amount of light they require; for example, the African violet (*Saintpaulia*) prefers some shade in summer, whereas pelargoniums revel in the sunlight. Blinds allow the gardener to provide and remove shading whenever necessary. Blinds may be fitted inside or outside the greenhouse and are invariably operated by hand; for this reason they have some of the same drawbacks as hand ventilation—for instance, when the gardener must be absent for any length of time.

Before fitting blinds it is as well to consider whether they are essential to the plants being grown. Many gardeners fit blinds to overcome wilting when in fact the problem lies in inadequate ventilation and/or unhealthy root growth.

Thermal screens

Any method of conserving heat is important in view of the steadily rising cost of fuels. I have already stressed the importance of light and the disadvantages of double glazing. The ideal is to have maximum light during daylight hours while preventing too much heat loss during the hours of darkness. This is the thinking behind the fitting of thermal screens, which are now being used increasingly by commercial growers. The screens act as a form of blanket over crops and their future adaptation to the amateur market is likely to come soon.

Pathways

It is very important to keep the greenhouse clean at all times, and good pathways can make a helpful contribution to this. Paths of hardened soil invariably encourage puddles to form when plants are watered and on clay soils the resultant slippery surface is both dangerous and messy. If the borders are used for crops, permanent pathways are not recommended because they can harbour soil pests and diseases. In such cases removable pathways are preferred; duckboards are cheap, but 50 mm (2 in) thick paving slabs look better, are simply laid straight on to the soil, and will take the weight of a loaded wheelbarrow without cracking. The pathway should continue for at least 1 m (3 ft) outside the greenhouse so that garden soil, which might contain harmful organisms, can be knocked off footwear before entering.

Keep the pathway as narrow as is practicable, for in most cases it is an unproductive area; a width of 450 to 600 mm (18 to 24 in) is about right for most situations.

Above left Thermal screens, widely used commercially (as here), may soon be available for domestic greenhouses. **Left** Internal or external adjustable blinds allow you to shade plants from direct sunlight. **Right** Paving stones make an attractive approach to the greenhouse and help prevent your bringing in garden soil on boots.

3 Planning

Few amateur gardeners devote all their greenhouse space to one crop. In the main, greenhouses are used for growing a variety of food and flower crops and so, as greater and greater demands are made on the available space, plants often suffer needlessly.

Advanced planning

Some simple forward planning is essential if you are to make the best possible use of your greenhouse. The first step is to decide what is to be the prime purpose of the greenhouse. This is easily said, but not so easily done. But it really is an essential decision – and once you have made it, you must put all other purposes firmly into second place. The prime purpose may fall into one of seven broad divisions:

(1) Growing pot plants for decoration in the greenhouse, conservatory, or in the home.

(2) Growing flowers for cutting – carnations, chrysanthemums, narcissus, and so on.

(3) Producing salad crops – lettuce, tomatoes, cucumbers, radishes, etc.

(4) Growing early vegetables entirely within the greenhouse – courgettes, carrots, early potatoes, and so on.

(5) Raising young plants for growing on out of doors – both bedding plants and vegetable plants.

(6) Growing fruit – peaches, strawberries, grapes, and so on.

(7) Plant propagation.

In practice, most people choose mixed cropping – that is, they grow prime-purpose crops plus a variety of other plants that require roughly similar growing conditions and for which space may from time to time become available. In planning the cropping programme, the first step is to calculate the growing area of border soil, benching, and shelving. The scale of the programme can then be worked out by referring to the amount of space required by an individual plant (this is set out in the chapters dealing with specific crops).

We can now look in more detail at each of the prime-purpose categories set out above, and consider some of the complementary crops that might be grown with them.

Pot plants for decoration

If these are grown as the main crop much of the space in the greenhouse or conservatory is likely to be taken up by permanent benching, and there will be little or no border space that receives direct sunlight. However, it should be possible to increase the cropping area in the spring months by installing temporary shelving which will be suitable for raising spring bedding plants and young vegetable plants. Beneath the benching, provided there is sufficient light, early potatoes may be chitted in boxes, dahlia tubers – also in boxes – started into growth, and chrysanthemum stools overwintered; some species of fern will also grow happily away from direct sunlight, and rhubarb may be forced in the darker areas.

The pot-plant programme can be geared either to producing plants at specific times – for example, in November and December and in the March-April period – or to providing some colour all the year round. If the aim is always to have available some specimen plants for the home, it is as well not to leave them too long in the house; refresh them from time to time by returning them to the greenhouse environment – and remember to set aside sufficient space for this to be done.

Above left Glass to the ground allows you to grow plants in the border soil. Draw up a cropping plan to make best use of the space, so that you neither overcrowd the plants nor waste this valuable growing area.

Glass to the ground allows sun-loving plants to be grown in the border soil on both sides. Small pot plants can be grown on shelving above.

One side partly bricked or boarded can be reserved for benching; shade-loving plants can be grown in the border soil beneath it.

If both sides are partly bricked, the end-wall border soil may be used (as here) for a large trained plant. Note cold frame on side wall.

Lean-to with vine trained up the main wall. When in full leaf, such plants reduce sunlight getting to the border soil beneath them.

Flowers for cutting

Chrysanthemums are probably the most widely grown cut flowers. It is not difficult to have them in bloom from September through to January provided the appropriate varieties are chosen and a little heat is available. Following on the propagation period in the spring, the plants are best left outdoors during the summer months, and rehoused in September just before the autumn frosts begin, The cut-flower grower with a little heat available may find that roses and carnations, grown either in pots or directly in the border soil, will happily complement chrysanthemums in his growing programme.

Salad crops

The main salad crops – lettuce, tomatoes, cucumbers, peppers, radishes, and spring onions – are grown in the greenhouse borders, and no benching is necessary. Tomatoes are one of the main summer crops and as such occupy the greenhouse from April or May through to September and even October. While the tomato plants are still small it is possible to grow a quick-maturing crop of early radishes between them. Although lettuces are often the crop to occupy the borders from October to April, their cultivation is not easy; but they mature at a time of high prices so they are well worth while. They can be cleared in time to allow you to prepare your borders for planting tomatoes. It is possible to get two crops of lettuce in winter in the south of England if soil-warming cables are used. To make the best use of the greenhouse, erect temporary shelving in the spring to provide propagating space for a wide range of other crops.

Salad crops grow particularly well in polythene-covered greenhouses, and today many gardeners buy this type solely for salad-crop production. They are especially useful if you wish to grow tomatoes and cucumbers. Under glass tomato plants and cucumber plants do not grow happily together because they require quite different humidity levels; in polythene-covered greenhouses, however, they usually grow satisfactorily side by side.

Plants raised in the greenhouse for subsequent planting outdoors need to be hardened-off in a garden frame. The amount of ventilation given is increased gradually until finally the top of the frame is left off.

Early vegetables

The development of the inexpensive polythene-covered greenhouse has caused a revival in the popularity of vegetable growing in the small garden area available in most modern homes. Provided suitable varieties are chosen, a wide range of vegetables can be grown without extra heating, and this intensive method allows more than one crop to be grown on the same ground. Filling the greenhouse borders with vegetables is no problem in the spring, summer, and autumn. In the winter months the choice is more limited; a crop of overwintering lettuces is one possibility, and rhubarb may be forced into growth if it is brought under cover in early January. If soil-warming cables are installed in part of the greenhouse border soil, even quicker growth can be achieved.

Polythene-covered structures are not usually designed to take shelving, and the manufacturer or retailer should be consulted if you want to install it. If their use is confined to the spring months, shelves should not be detrimental to the crops beneath.

Plants for growing on outdoors

Few home gardeners devote their greenhouses solely to this specialized sector of plant propagation, but it is an important and rewarding greenhouse activity. For the bedding-plant enthusiast the greenhouse will be used in the spring months to raise the summer-bedding plants – antirrhinums, lobelia, alyssum, begonias, ageratum, phlox, and the like. Space must be set aside for propagation by cuttings of plants such as dahlias, geraniums, and fuchsias, and temporary benching and shelving may be necessary. If you intend to raise young plants, remember that your programme will clash with plans to raise under glass a wide range of young vegetable plants – early lettuce, runner beans, summer cauliflowers, marrows, and courgettes. Vegetable plants raised in the greenhouse crop much earlier than those raised outdoors.

For this type of programme a garden frame is essential, for the young plants will need to be hardened off before they are planted in open ground. They are moved to the closed frame upon reaching a suitable size. The amount of ventilation given is then increased by stages until the plants become adjusted to outdoor conditions.

In the summer months, after the young plants have been planted out, the greenhouse can be devoted to tomatoes. Alternatives to this use are limited but one of the best is to grow half-hardy plants in pots for display purposes; tall-growing antirrhinums in flower look particularly fine. An alternative border crop might be chrysanthemums planted where they are to flower. This prime-purpose category tends to leave the greenhouse underemployed over the winter months. But if you intend to propagate from various flowering plants, such as fuchsia and pelargonium, the following year, you should make provision for overwintering them in frost-free conditions in the greenhouse.

Fruit

Now that good imported fruit is widely available one rarely sees a greenhouse devoted mainly to the cultivation of peaches or grapes, as in bygone years. However, fan-trained peaches may be grown against the back wall of lean-tos and will provide good crops of fruit as long as they are tended carefully. They take up relatively little space, require no additional heat, and leave the remainder of the greenhouse for growing other crops.

A vine, on the other hand, will take up a lot of greenhouse space within a year or two, and although it normally grows in the roof area the large leaves cut out much light and so give poor growing conditions beneath. The vine is certainly not a plant to be recommended if space is limited or if the gardener is anxious to grow a range of other plants as well. Both peaches and vines prefer unheated conditions during the dormant (winter) period, and ventilators should be left open a little. Consequently few crops are suitable for growing alongside them during this period of the year.

Early strawberries are fast becoming a popular fruit to grow in the greenhouse. Once commonly grown one plant per pot, alternative ways are now finding favour. Growing in pockets in vertical, tube-like containers standing on the floor allows many plants to be cultivated in a small area, and the plants are in the greenhouse only for a few weeks in the spring – though regrettably at a time when the greenhouse is already bulging with other young plants. Early strawberries are consequently best introduced into other cropping programmes as and when space allows.

Plant propagation is discussed in detail in Chapter 7.

Peach tree in blossom in a commercial greenhouse. The drawing shows how to fan-train a peach tree with the help of bamboo canes. A peach tree looks attractive against the end wall of the greenhouse, leaving space in borders and benching.

4 Flowering and Foliage Plants

THE majority of flowering and foliage plants are grown not in the border soil but in containers of one kind or another. The medium in which they grow has to provide food for the plant as well as anchorage, and the major elements and trace elements have to be present in the right proportions to produce a plant that will remain healthy for weeks, months, and even years. During this time it may be subjected to the equivalent of several hundred millimetres of rainfall, and ordinary garden soil cannot satisfactorily stand up to these artificial conditions; in many cases garden soil completely loses its structure within a short time and sets hard on drying. The plant first begins to look off colour; later the leaves start to yellow and flower buds drop off. If the plant is removed from its container the roots may look dark brown, have a pungent smell, and show no sign of active growth. The plant dies mainly as a result of a lack of available food and of air to the roots.

Growing mediums

LOAM COMPOSTS Special growing mediums have been developed for container-grown greenhouse plants, and the more important ones are described in this chapter. For over 50 years the John Innes composts have been used by commercial growers and amateur gardeners alike. The name John Innes is taken from the research station where they were formulated after years of investigative work. The formulations provide horticulturists with various growing mediums to cover every greenhouse activity, from seed sowing through to final potting. All these formulations are based on the use of good loam. They have stood the test of time, and composts made up to the original formulae are available at most horticultural stores and garden centres.

There are, however, many gardeners who prefer to mix their own composts and the brief description here will provide guidance as to what is entailed. Kettering loam is a medium heavy loam, and while this is ideal it is not readily available in all parts of the country and a similar loam may have to be used instead. The term 'loam' here means the top 75 to 100 mm (3 to 4 in) of a grass field. After cutting, the sods are placed grass downwards in a rectangular stack about 1.5 m ($4\frac{1}{2}$ ft) square. The stack is watered well while it is being built, and a layer of rotted farmyard manure or similar is spread at 150 mm (6 in) intervals throughout. The stack is finished off at a height of 1 to 1.5 m (3 ft to $4\frac{1}{2}$ ft) and a polythene sheet is placed over the top to keep off excessive rain. After some six months the stack may be used as required by slicing down one face with a spade and putting the loam through a riddle. The result is a fibrous soil which to the experienced gardener looks good, feels good, and even smells good! However, it may unfortunately contain pests and diseases injurious to plants, as well as weed seeds. For these reasons it has to be partially sterilized at a temperature not exceeding 82°C (180°F) with no part of the 'cooking' being below 71°C (163°F). This is best done in a small electric sterilizer which passes steam through the loam, killing all the harmful organisms in about an hour. The 'cooked' loam may be used after two weeks. It is then mixed with peat, a coarse sand or grit, lime (chalk), and a base fertilizer in the following proportions (by volume):

JOHN INNES SEED COMPOST

2 parts loam
1 part peat
1 part coarse sand

To each bushel (0.04 cu m) of this mixture is added 20 g ($\frac{3}{4}$ oz) chalk and 40 g ($1\frac{1}{2}$ oz) superphosphate.

Above left Three popular potting composts: peat-based, peat and sand, and loam-based. **Right** The flower grower can have colour in the greenhouse all the year round.

JOHN INNES POTTING COMPOST No. 1
7 parts loam
3 parts peat
2 parts sand

To each bushel (0.04 cu m) of this mixture is added 20 g (¾ oz) chalk and 115 g (4 oz) of John Innes Base Fertilizer (a mixture of hoof-and-horn meal, superphosphate, and potassium sulphate) which is sold ready for use. J.I. Potting Compost No. 2 is the same as No. 1 but with an extra 115 g (4 oz) of Base Fertilizer; Potting Compost No. 3 is the same as No. 1 but with an extra 230 g (8 oz) of Base Fertilizer. Do not mix too large a quantity at any one time: it is best used within six to eight weeks.

All composts need to be kept where they will not be contaminated by weed seeds, soil, already used compost, or unclean pots; harmful bacteria from these sources can quickly infect the sterilized compost. It is highly desirable to establish a clean (sterilized) area in the greenhouse and to make it a rule never to move used pots, seed trays, and so on into the area until they have been thoroughly washed and allowed to drain. Too often, equipment is carefully sterilized – and then left to collect weeds and disease organisms. It is little wonder that gardeners who treat their equipment in this way often complain that expensive composts have failed to produce healthy plants.

LOAMLESS COMPOSTS In recent years loamless composts based on mixtures of peat and sand or on peat alone have become increasingly popular. Their attraction stems from the fact that the ideal loam is difficult to obtain, the sterilizing process is laborious and costly, and the weight of readymade J.I. composts leads to high carriage costs. The components of loamless composts are sterile to start with and the composts are considerably lighter in weight. The amateur gardener should buy such composts ready-mixed, for peats and sands vary and not all are suitable for seed and potting mixtures.

Gardeners accustomed to using loam-based composts will initially find peat/sand composts more difficult to manage. They need to be moist to start with, and if they dry out they are difficult to re-wet. Also, because they are light in weight, tall plants can more easily tip or be blown over along with the container in which they are growing; this can be overcome by putting a little J.I. compost in the bottom of the pot to weigh it down.

Plant pots and seed containers are made in a variety of materials for different uses.

Seeds germinate more rapidly in peat and peat/sand mixtures than in loam composts, and the light, open texture of such mixtures seems also to suit many mature plants – most proprietary growing bags are filled with them. Feeding of container-grown plants needs to begin earlier with loamless composts than with loam composts. On the other hand, there is no need to line the bottom of pots with crocks if peat/sand composts are used, and they are specially suitable if plants are to be watered by capillary action – for example, by means of a tray of moistened sand placed under the pots.

Pots

As most greenhouse flowering plants are grown in pots, I should perhaps make a few general observations about these containers. Pots are available in a great variety of sizes, shapes, and materials. The size of a pot is defined not by its height but by the inside diameter of the rim. The range of standard sizes includes 65 mm (2½ in), 90 mm (3½ in), 130 mm (5 in), and 180 mm (7 in); the so-called half-pots (half the height of normal pots) are also available in standard sizes. The materials of construction include flexible and rigid plastic, clay (earthenware), whalehide, papier-mâché, and peat.

The longest-lasting types are those of plastic and clay. The former, whether flexible or rigid, are lighter than clay pots, are easier to clean, and are available in a range of colours. Many gardeners, however, prefer the appearance of clay pots. In purely horticultural terms neither type is better than the other, but it is important to remember that they provide somewhat different environments for the potting mixture. Clay is porous and tends to absorb the moisture in the compost; plastic pots are impermeable (non-porous), so plants growing in them need to be watered less (or less often) in the greenhouse. However, exactly the opposite applies when pots are 'plunged'. This term means to take potted plants out of the greenhouse and bury them in a prepared hole in the garden to a depth that enables the rims of the pots to be covered by about 25 mm (1 in) of soil. Under these circumstances, clay pots will take up moisture from the surrounding soil, helping to keep the potting compost adequately moist, but impermeable plastic pots resist the passage of water, and the moisture of the compost of plunged plants in such pots must be checked more often in dry weather. For these reasons it is sensible to make a firm decision to use either plastic or clay pots, not both; this is also important if you intend to use automatic or semi-automatic watering systems. New clay pots, incidentally, should be soaked in water for 48 hours and allowed to drain thoroughly before being used.

Whalehide pots are made from a form of thin, specially treated cardboard that is colour-coded according to durability. Red ones have a useful life of up to one year; black ones (like papier-mâché pots) will last only for a couple of months or so.

Peat pots are used when seedlings need to be grown on for a few weeks before potting on (transferring to larger, permanent pots) or planting in greenhouse border soil or outdoors. The peat allows the plant roots to grow through the walls of the pot and, in both potting on and planting out, the plant and its peat pot are transferred as one to the new growing medium.

The potting of plants is a less simple matter than many inexperienced gardeners realize. One of the commonest mistakes is to use too big a pot. Young plants should always be started off on the smallest size possible and then potted on as soon as their roots begin to crowd the available space. This applies especially to flowering plants, because under-potting tends to assist flower development, while over-potting encourages greater leaf growth. Seedlings and small plants, then, should be potted initially in a 90 mm ($3\frac{1}{2}$ in) pot. Make sure that the fresh compost completely envelops the roots; then settle the compost around the roots by putting the newly potted plant sharply down on the bench. Apply a little water but do not make the compost sodden. When potting on becomes necessary, select the next size up – 130 mm (5 in) – rather than a larger pot. Because the plant is likely to remain longer in the bigger pot, put some crocks (pieces of a broken clay pot) or pebbles at the bottom of the pot before adding fresh compost. This will allow excess water to drain away easily. Potting on should always be done with care to avoid damaging the root ball – the tangled mass of roots and soil.

Above Making a plunge bed. Dig a trench slightly wider and deeper than the pots. Fill the space between the pots with moist ash, coarse sand, or peat, then cover up pot rims with a thin layer of soil. **Below** Potting on. Put a few crocks in the bottom of the new pot, then partly fill it with growing compost. Insert the plant, adding more compost around the root ball.

Preparing border soil

This work is described in detail in Chapter 6, since the border soil is used more extensively in the growing of food crops than of flowering plants. The main difference is in the use of fertilizers. Generally speaking, high-nitrogen fertilizers should not be used with flowering plants because they stimulate leaf growth. 'Complete' (NPK) fertilizers should be high in phosphates and potash and low in nitrogen. Most flowering plants flourish in a slightly acid soil of *p*H 6.5.

Capillary benching

This is the term used to describe benching constructed so as to allow plants growing in pots to be watered automatically. The bench becomes in effect a trough of water, the level of which is critically controlled by the water being 'absorbed' into a matting covering or a layer of sand. The compost in the plant pots must establish good contact with this surface, so all crocks must be removed from the bottom of the pots. When setting out the plants press each one firmly on to the bench. If capillarity is not established, place a small 'wick' in the base of the pot; this will draw up water into the compost.

Benching of this type copes satisfactorily with pots of different sizes and with plants requiring differing amounts of water, so it is a boon for the amateur gardener who is away from home during the day.

Heating

The range of flowering plants that can be grown and the make-up of the year-round cropping programme will depend on the minimum greenhouse temperature the amateur gardener is prepared to maintain. I have already mentioned the fact that even the more hardy greenhouse plants are likely to succumb to disease if temperatures remain only one or two degrees above freezing point for any length of time. A much more ambitious growing programme can be contemplated if the greenhouse is kept at a minimum temperature of 7°C (45°F). This I shall refer to henceforward as the 'cool' greenhouse. It is becoming increasingly popular with greenhouse growers and will feature largely in the notes that follow on specific plants.

Moving up the scale to the 'warm' greenhouse involves maintaining a minimum of 12°C (53°F), which further broadens the cropping spectrum of flowering and foliage plants; but the cost of maintaining such a temperature in the winter months is considerable. The hot-house, with an overall minimum temperature of 18 to 20°C (65 to 68°F) is almost a thing of the past in amateur gardening and for this reason is not dealt with here. However, local temperatures as high as this are required during the propagation period of many greenhouse flowering and foliage plants, and can be economically obtained by using a propagating box or frame.

In practice most greenhouse owners will be aiming for a mixed cropping programme – food crops along with flowering and foliage plants. Each individual will have his or her own preferences and the resultant mix will call for compromises in growing conditions. Some simple year-round plan is essential to prevent chaos in the greenhouse, the cold frames, and associated areas.

Growing methods

The following is a selection of flowering and foliage plants commonly grown in the greenhouse by amateur gardeners. There are, of course, hundreds of such plants suitable for growing under glass or plastic, but space allows us to deal with only a few. The selection is, however, varied enough to plan a range of alternative programmes, including mixed cropping with food plants (*see* Chapter 6).

Each pot plant should be regularly examined for signs of pests and diseases.

Asparagus Ferns

Suitable for growing in the cool greenhouse, the asparagus ferns are half-hardy perennials renowned for their attractive foliage. *A. plumosus nanus* has slender, delicate foliage much used by florists as a background for buttonhole flowers; the dark green needle-like foliage of *A. sprengeri*, with its pendulous habit, is liked both by flower arrangers and by hanging-basket enthusiasts.

Asparagus ferns are normally grown in pots in John Innes Potting Compost No. 3 (JIP3) or in a soil-less compost. Frequency of feeding during the summer growing season will depend to some extent on whether the foliage is being cut or the plants are allowed to grow without disturbance. In the former case use a general fertilizer with a high nitrogen content. As the plants grow in size, pot on into 130 mm (5 in) pots. For propagation, the plants may be divided in March or, alternatively, raised from seed in early spring in temperatures of around 20°C (68°F).

Delicate foliage of *Asparagus plumosus* fern.

Camellias

Although camellias grow satisfactorily out of doors in southern parts of England, they develop the finest blooms when grown in the greenhouse. They need little or no applied heat, and if suitable varieties are selected they will provide beautiful pink, red, or white flowers from October through to April. When the young rooted plants are received they may be potted straight into 130 mm (5 in) clay pots using a lime-free compost; if you prepare your own John Innes formulation, omit the chalk. If a loamless compost is used, ensure that it is of a type suitable for acid-loving plants.

The plants are normally grown out of doors from the late spring through to early autumn; it is best to plunge them in their pots in an ash bed. If this is done they will require regular watering, but the risk of their drying out (which can cause buds to drop off many months later) will be reduced. Being evergreen the leaves will get dirty unless syringed regularly, and soft water should be used for this; in hard-water districts use rainwater both for syringing and for normal watering.

When camellias have finished flowering they should be lightly pruned to maintain their shape. Pot on when necessary.

The lovely *Camellia* 'Waltz Time'.

Carnations

The perpetual-flowering *Dianthus* varieties are hardy and will grow well with the minimum of heat, giving blooms for most of the year. Carnations prefer a cool, airy greenhouse – which is why those who exhibit them regularly grow them on their own. Well-grown plants will reach a height of more than 2 m (6 ft) and so must usually be grown in a greenhouse with glass right down to the ground.

It is best to buy young rooted plants early in the year, so that you start with clean, healthy stock. The nurseryman should have 'stopped' the plants (removed the growing tip) before despatching them to you, in order to encourage the side shoots to develop. On arrival they should be potted into 90 mm (3½ in) pots. Later, before they become pot-bound, they will need potting on into 180 mm (7 in) pots, using JIP3 or a loamless compost. By this time the side shoots will probably be about 130 mm (5 in) long, and they in turn will need stopping by removal of the growing tips. The side shoots grow at different rates, so stop the fastest-growing one first to prevent them all flowering at the same time.

From then on the plants will grow steadily if regularly provided with a proprietary liquid feed. They need support from an early stage and four canes per pot will be required when they have been transferred to the 180 mm (7 in) pots; alternatively, you can use the neat purpose-made carnation supports sold by most sundriesmen.

Disbudding is necessary to get worthwhile flowers, so as soon as you can see that the terminal or crown bud is undamaged remove the buds that form immediately beneath it. Removal of the flowering bloom with its stem is a form of pruning, and it only remains to train in new growths. Perpetual-flowering varieties provide a continuous succession of blooms for two years or more. It is then best to destroy the plants and start afresh.

Some types of carnations can be grown from seed sown in the propagating frame early in the year. As they grow they may be potted into small pots or widely spaced in boxes. If planted out in open ground in April–May they will flower in August. In mid-September, if carefully lifted and placed in pots in the cool greenhouse, they will continue to provide colour throughout the winter months. Many of the varieties are scented.

Popular border carnation 'Alice Forbes'.

Chrysanthemums grow in a cool greenhouse.

Chrysanthemums

Chrysanthemums are likely to form the basis of many cropping programmes because they do not occupy the greenhouse for what can often be its busiest time, from May to mid-September. They rate highly as a value-for-money plant: they give a lot of colour over a long period, and they are relatively hardy and versatile. Depending on variety they may be grown simply as decorative plants in the borders, as short pot plants, or in pots for exhibition purposes. (The National Chrysanthemum Society classifies indoor varieties as Large Exhibition, with petals incurving and reflexing, Medium Exhibition, Exhibition Incurved, Reflexed Decoratives, and Intermediate Decoratives.) Cool greenhouse temperatures are adequate for all types.

CULTIVATION Most chrysanthemums are propagated by means of cuttings and, when starting, the greenhouse gardener would be well advised to buy young rooted plants from a specialist raiser. In this way he is assured of getting healthy young plants, virus-free and true to type. If he looks after them properly he can propagate his own plants from these in future years.

On arrival in March or April the young plants are potted up into 90 mm ($3\frac{1}{2}$ in) pots using JIP1 or a soil-less compost. They will need some warmth initially and space should be found on shelving where they will get a reasonable amount of direct sunlight. Unless they are being treated as lifted chrysanthemums, it will be necessary to pot on into 130 mm (5 in) pots before the plants get pot-bound; as they are vigorous growers, this stage may be reached in four to five weeks. If you are using a loam-based compost it is usual to compress the soil rather more than one would normally do: 'pot firmly' is the

Potted chrysanthemums: 1 Rooted cutting in a 90 mm (3½ in) pot; 2 The break bud; 3 First crown buds; 4 Second crown buds; 5 Pinching out a growing tip.

advice often given to beginners. In the bigger pots the plants take up a substantial amount of room, so they should be moved to a cold frame as soon as they have settled down after potting on. They must not get frosted in the frame, so if a cold night is expected cover the plants with sheets of newspaper.

In June the plants are moved into still larger pots – 180 or 220 mm (7 or 8½ in) – and stood out, 75 to 100 mm (3 to 4 in) apart, on boards or slates. Here they remain until they are returned to the greenhouse in mid-September.

Many amateurs will prefer to adopt a less elaborate system. Lifted chrysanthemums, for instance, are quite suitable for decorative purposes. The plants, in 90 mm (3½ in) pots, are moved to the cold frame to harden off. In May they are planted 380 mm (15 in) apart in well-prepared ground out of doors. Here they remain until mid-September, when they are lifted with care from their summer quarters and transferred with as much soil as possible into the greenhouse border. I like to prepare the plants for this move by driving in the blade of a spade to its full depth around half the plant, and some 130 mm (5 in) from it, five weeks before lifting, a fortnight later repeating this around the other half of the plant.

Left alone, a young chrysanthemum plant with one or more pairs of leaves will develop a bud at its apex which will not form a flower; this is known as a break bud. From the axils of the leaves below this bud, young shoots will appear – a phenomenon known as a 'natural break'. The buds that form are called first crown buds. They may abort in turn and the process will be repeated, with the flowers forming on the next lot of buds; these are called second crown buds. The timing of flowering and the number and size of blooms are affected by this process. In practice, some manipulation by pinching out is usually necessary and a good chrysanthemum catalogue will make recommendations for each variety.

As a rule the greenhouse decorative varieties carry their flowers on second crown buds. The gardener does not wait for the break bud to form but pinches out the growing tip of the plant while it is still in its first pot and is 150 to 230 mm (6 to 9 in) tall. When these growths are about 250 mm (10 in) long – probably in late May or early June – they, too, must have their growing tip removed, three or four side shoots being allowed to develop on each stem, and any other shoots which develop being rubbed off.

After flowering the plants should be cut down to about 450 mm (18 in) in height and a number selected to provide cuttings for the future. To save space it is best to label each plant individually and then to box them closely together in a 100 mm (4 in) deep box, sifting potting compost between them. In January you should reduce their height to 75 mm (3 in). Shoots will then soon begin to grow. Exhibition varieties will need to be propagated in January and February, and decorative varieties in February and March. The plants will happily overwinter in the cool greenhouse provided they do not remain wet for long periods.

PESTS AND DISEASES The fungus disease known as 'damping off' can be a tricky problem with greenhouse chrysanthemums; the blooms of soft plants that have received high-nitrogen feeds are particularly prone to it. The disease is greatly encouraged by wide fluctuations in temperature and by high humidity. Try to maintain the temperature at a steady 7 to 10°C (45 to 51°F); on damp days keep the air circulating throughout the greenhouse (but beware of draughts). Of the pests, aphids are troublesome, leaf miners deface the foliage, and earwigs damage the young shoots and eat the petals. Eelworm can be serious if the plants are grown in the garden soil.

Above Potted *Cyclamen persicum* hybrids in flower. **Right** *Fuchsia* 'Royal Velvet' makes an attractive centrepiece of a hanging basket.

Cyclamen

In spite of the length of time between seed sowing and flowering, cyclamen are justly popular and can be grown in the cool greenhouse. They are available in a wide range of colours, with plain or variegated foliage, and some varieties are scented.

Plants for Christmas are sown from September to November for flowering the following year. Propagation temperatures of about 17°C (63°F) are best, and the young plants, one to each 90 mm (3½ in) pot, are overwintered at a minimum temperature of 15°C (59°F). To heat the whole greenhouse to this temperature would be expensive, so plan to let the plants remain in their propagating quarters as long as possible – certainly until April. About this time pot on into 130 mm (5 in) pots, using JIP3 or a loamless compost. Once the plants have established themselves after potting on, they should be transferred to a lightly shaded cold frame. On warm days in summer the cold frame should be ventilated freely; this will encourage the development of compact plants without loose, straggly foliage. Return the plants to the greenhouse in September.

Seed may also be sown in spring, and the plants later potted into 90 mm (3½ in) pots in which they are allowed to flower. Flowering will continue for several weeks, after which watering should be gradually reduced in order to dry off the corm (the swollen stem base). Corms may be restarted into growth in July and August in fresh compost. Make sure after re-potting that the top half of each corm is above the surface of the compost – if planted too deep the corms tend to rot. Cyclamen grown from corms in this manner should be discarded after the summer flowering.

Fuchsias

With its graceful pendulous flowers the fuchsia deserves a place in every mixed collection of greenhouse plants, for it provides colour over a period of many months. Although it is widely grown as a pot plant, it also looks well in hanging baskets and is attractive when grown as a standard.

The greenhouse varieties will over-winter satisfactorily in a minimum temperature of 5°C (42°F) and may be put outside in their pots for the warmer summer months. They are normally propagated by cuttings of new growth taken in the spring, but can also be raised from seed; in the latter case it is usual to propagate those it is desired to retain by cuttings.

Specialist firms list many named varieties in their catalogues and rooted cuttings are despatched in the spring. A good way of starting is to buy a named collection. Upon receipt pot them into 90 mm (3½ in) pots and spray them regularly with water to help them become established. Plants destined for hanging baskets may be moved straight from these pots into their new quarters; two or three should be planted around the edge of each basket. Plants for flowering in the greenhouse will need to be potted on into 130 mm (5 in) pots in due course. The removal of the growing tip may be necessary at this stage if side growths have been slow to develop. These plants will need feeding throughout the flowering period. In late autumn the amount of water is reduced and the plants shed their leaves; some cutting back of the plant, and removal of weak shoots, will reduce the amount of space they will take up in the greenhouse over the winter.

Plants to be grown as standards should have a strong-growing central leader. When they are moved into 130 mm (5 in) pots a 1.5 m (5 ft) garden cane is inserted into the pot and the leading growth secured loosely to this. Lateral growths are pinched out until the main stem reaches the desired height, usually just over 1 m (3 ft), when they are encouraged to develop laterally and form a balanced head to the plant. Fuchsias may take two growing seasons to reach this stage. The larger standards will probably require potting on into 180 mm (7 in) pots in later years.

Hardy Ferns

There are numerous species of hardy ferns, most of them graceful plants which grow well in any greenhouse with a mixed cropping programme. When in pots they are ideal for setting off small displays of flowering plants, although generally speaking ferns like to have a free root run and will therefore grow better when they are planted in the border soil. They also look well in troughs, either free-standing or against a wall.

The ferns' natural habitats are shady places, and they do not like full sunlight; but they will grow in partial shade, and most of them will tolerate the conditions found beneath benching as long as some light is available. The rosy maidenhair *Adiantum hispidulum* is evergreen when grown in the cool greenhouse. If space is short it may be grown outdoors in sheltered situations so long as it is hardened off properly. Unlike many ferns it will tolerate full sun and is consequently ideal for bench-growing. *Asplenium bulbiferum* is a popular greenhouse fern which grows best in the border soil; some varieties will tolerate the cold and grow in an unheated greenhouse. The fronds of the fern carry small bulbs, or bulbils (whence the species name), and young plantlets; these plantlets can be removed and used for propagation. Avoid overhead watering of aspleniums, as it may lead to rotting. The ribbon or brake fern *Pteris cretica,* one of the smaller species, is suitable both for the unheated or cool greenhouse and for the home. It makes an excellent centrepiece in larger hanging baskets, where its long, graceful fronds are shown off to advantage.

Ferns grow best in lime-free soils. If you plan to use a loamless or John Innes compost make sure it is a mixture suitable for acid-loving plants. Potting on can usually be done at the beginning of the growing season every year. Only rainwater should be used for watering or overhead spraying. Ferns are propagated from spores, best sown in the warmer part of the year.

Asplenium bulbiferum is one of many species of hardy ferns that will grow in border soil that is partly shaded by benching.

Hydrangeas

Well-grown hydrangeas are big plants, and some gardeners consider they look out of place in a small greenhouse. Certainly they may upset the balance of a mixed stand of plants; on the other hand, they are hardy and grow well in a cool greenhouse and have the advantage of occupying greenhouse space only in the winter and early spring months. *Hydrangea macrophylla* and its varieties that make up the Hortensia group are probably the most popular of this type, producing clusters of showy but infertile flowers built up into large globular heads in a wide range of colours and sizes, including pink, white, red, and blue. Another popular type is the lacecap hydrangea, whose flower head is flat with an outer ring of false petals enclosing small florets.

Propagation is by cuttings taken in February and March from flowering shoots and rooted in a propagating frame in a temperature of about 18°C (65°F). After rooting, the plants are potted into 90 mm ($3\frac{1}{2}$ in) pots using a lime-free compost. Once established, the growing tip is removed above the second pair of leaves. In early summer they are potted on into 130 mm (5 in) clay pots using a lime-free JIP3 or loamless compost; the newly potted plants are stood in a frame to harden off for a few days, then plunged outside. Around midsummer's day the side shoots that have developed should also be stopped above the second pair of leaves to provide a framework for a well-shaped plant. Regular watering and feeding of plunged hydrangeas is essential.

The plants should be returned to the greenhouse in autumn after they have shed their leaves; at this stage they prefer cool temperatures. In late winter, as the days lengthen and day temperatures begin to rise, hydrangeas come into flower in the cool greenhouse and provide colour for many weeks. After blossoming, the flowering stems should be cut back hard. In early summer the plants are again plunged outside, for the cycle to be repeated.

Hydrangea macrophylla makes a fine pot plant, but because of its size it is more suited to the bigger greenhouse.

Orchids

The orchid family accounts for almost one sixth of all the flowering-plant species. Although orchids were for long widely regarded as hot-house plants, many will grow in a cool greenhouse. Of these, *Cymbidium*, *Odontoglossum*, *Miltonia*, and *Paphiopedilum* (formerly *Cypripedium*) species and some others are nowadays within the realm of the average amateur gardener.

Cymbidium will provide sprays of flowers in the spring. *Odontoglossum* (evergreen) flower in spring and summer. Some securing of the pseudo-bulb – the swollen base of the stem – to the container with a fine wire may be necessary. The many species of *Miltonia* will provide flowers throughout the summer. *Paphiopedilum* differ from the above in that they have no pseudo-bulbs; they flower after growth has finished, and propagation is by division.

Orchids are not widely grown by nurserymen and it is usual to purchase plants from orchid specialists. The fine exhibits staged at many shows provide an opportunity to compare named varieties, but their high cost deters many would-be growers. Initially it may be better to buy the less expensive seedlings and gain experience with them, although it will often be 12 to 18 months before they come into flower.

Take the advice of a knowledgeable supplier when selecting plants for the cool greenhouse; the genera mentioned above include species that will overwinter happily if a minimum temperature of 7°C (45°F) can be maintained. However, problems can arise in greenhouses with mixed cropping programmes, because on very hot days in the summer months the orchids will need to be protected from the direct rays of the sun and the high temperatures. It may be best to move them for a time to an unused deep garden frame, which can be shaded and ventilated to provide the optimum conditions, rather than upset the other plants.

The cultivation of orchids differs somewhat from that of the usual run of greenhouse plants. An open compost of various mixtures of fibrous peat, sphagnum moss, and leaf mould was once recommended, but this is now being replaced by proprietary composts incorporating synthetic materials. The plants may be grown on a bench but are often grown in wire baskets or pans suspended from the glazing bars. They require no feeding but need repotting every two years. Water them regularly with rainwater in the summer months but keep them on the dry side during the winter months.

Above The orchid *Miltonia* 'Knight Errant' provides flowers throughout the summer.
Right *Passiflora caerulea racemosa*, an attractive climbing plant that is propagated by cuttings taken in spring or early summer or by seed sown in heat in February or March.

Passion Flower

The passion flower (*Passiflora caerulea*) is an attractive climbing plant suitable for growing in a cool greenhouse, or even in an unheated one in the warmer parts of the country. It carries numerous flat, open, star-like flowers of white, blue, and purple during the summer and is a half-hardy perennial usually raised from seed sown in heat in February or March. Germination is not always rapid and can take up to six weeks. When the seedlings are large enough to handle, pot them into 90 mm ($3\frac{1}{2}$ in) pots and later into 130 mm (5 in) pots. In autumn the plants may be moved either into the greenhouse border or into large pots or tubs in readiness for flowering the following year.

Train the shoots up a light wire framework; they will eventually grow up to 5 m (16 ft) in length. They are not heavy, however, and do not cut out too much light. Pruning, in February, consists of removing the weak shoots and shortening the previous year's growth on the remaining shoots by about one third.

Propagation is also possible by taking cuttings of young shoots in the spring and early summer; they are not difficult to root in a propagating case.

Pelargoniums

Pelargoniums are high on most people's list of popular greenhouse plants, for the flowering types provide colour throughout the summer and in some cases well into the autumn. They may be classified as 'zonal', with leaf margins of a different colour from the main colour of the leaf (these are commonly called 'geraniums'); 'show', which are widely grown for their attractive semi-double flowers; 'fancy', somewhat smaller versions of show pelargoniums; 'ivy-leafed', with attractive ivy-shaped leaves, sometimes variegated, which trail or climb and are consequently ideal for incorporating in hanging baskets; and 'scented-leaved', grown mainly for their scent.

It has been customary to propagate pelargoniums from cuttings taken in July and August, but owing to poor selection some stocks have deteriorated over the years. Leading commercial growers have made strenuous efforts to improve the quality of plants, but with the introduction of F_1 hybrids, raised from seed sown in heat in January, many amateur gardeners have taken to raising their own. Seeds need to be in temperatures of 21 to 22°C (70 to 73°F) to germinate, and such temperatures are attained without difficulty in a small propagating frame. Once potted in 90 mm (3½ in) pots they grow on satisfactorily in lower temperatures. Highly commended by the Royal Horticultural Society are the 'Carefree' hybrids, which ultimately grow to a height of 450 mm (18 in), and the somewhat shorter 'Sprinter' has been internationally acclaimed.

A few standard plants are always useful for display purposes and the show types are not difficult to train. Select strong-growing young plants and remove all side growths. Tie the single stem that remains to a cane; it will grow to a height of at least 600 mm (2 ft) in the first year. Before they recommence growth in the second year move the plants to bigger pots and allow the single stem to continue growing up to the required height: a clean stem of just over 1 m (3 ft) makes for a useful plant. Once this height has been attained side shoots are again allowed to develop. Prune the top of the plant annually to keep an open framework, but on no account put the knife into the main stem.

Roses

Commercial growers devote a considerable acreage of glasshouse space to roses, which are grown in the border soil and remain *in situ* for several years. Requiring minimum temperatures in winter of 7 to 10°C (45 to 51°F), the rose is suitable for growing in the home greenhouse in pots, not the border.

Bare-rooted plants should be purchased from a rose grower early in the lifting season, possibly November, and his help should be sought in choosing first-quality plants with a strong growth. It is best to avoid container-grown plants, which may have been potted into a compost unsuitable for a long spell of intensive growing. Any field soil that remains on the roots will need to be washed off and the plant potted into a 200 mm (8 in) clay pot using JIP3 or a loamless compost; with the former, good drainage must be provided. Some root trimming may be necessary to fit the roots into the pot; any cuts should be made cleanly using a sharp knife.

Prune the plants before they are brought into the warmth at the turn of the year, when a maximum temperature of 10°C (51°F) should not be exceeded. There will be some flowers in the first spring flush, but considerably more in later years. Plunge the plants outside in their pots for the summer and autumn months and rehouse them earlier in the second and subsequent years. As is the case with all plants grown in containers, liquid feeding is important and feeds with a high potash content are best used at and near flowering time.

Bulbs

A large number of flowering plants can be grown from bulbs in the greenhouse. Perhaps the most popular among amateur growers are narcissi, tulips, and hyacinths, all of which will thrive under 'cool' greenhouse conditions. Choose any of the fine modern varieties of each, but avoid planting bulbs of different varieties in the same containers. The earliest-flowering are the 'prepared' bulbs, but they are more expensive owing to the temperature-controlled conditions in which they have to be stored after lifting. Earliness is, indeed, their only advantage: the quality of their flowers is in no way superior to that of normal bulbs, which in any case will bloom much earlier in the greenhouse than specimens planted in the garden.

Buy big bulbs for greenhouse flowering, and pot them in September or November in the recommended composts. The depth of the container is important, because there should be at least 25 mm (1 in) of compost below the base of the bulbs. The top quarter of the bulbs can rise above the surface of the compost without affecting their eventual flowering performance. Clay pots are the most attractive containers for these flowers. On the other hand, more or less any type of suitably shaped container is satisfactory if you are growing bulbs to provide cut flowers (I have used well-washed fish boxes with success). Whatever containers you use, make sure that they provide good drainage.

After potting, water the bulbs well. Then plunge them outdoors in a sheltered position, covering them with a 25 mm (1 in) layer of peat, and heap about 100 mm (4 in) of garden soil on top. When the plants have developed a good growth of foliage, bring them into the greenhouse. The foliage will need supporting; small twigs are adequate for narcissi, but use split bamboo canes for tulips and hyacinths. After flowering, the bulbs may be planted out in the garden.

Inexpensive Flowering Plants

A wide range of greenhouse plants may be raised from seed. As only a few plants are normally required they are sown in pans and germinated in heat in the propagating frame. The usual routine is initially to pot the more vigorous seedlings direct into 90 mm (3½ in) pots, and to prick out the weaker ones into boxes where they are allowed to grow on for a while before they are potted for the first time.

As the plants grow and the roots fill the pot, a second potting into 130 mm (5 in) pots is made and most plants will perform perfectly well in this size of pot. Liquid feeding of the plants is important, especially during the periods of rapid growth. With loamless composts it is important that feeding begins early. Some popular examples of this group are described overleaf.

Potting on pelargoniums into 125 mm (5 in) pots for a summer display in the greenhouse.

Antirrhinum majus 'Madame Butterfly' makes an outstanding display under glass, with flower spikes up to 1 m (3 ft) long.

ANTIRRHINUM The snapdragons are normally associated with schemes of garden bedding, but when grown in pots in the greenhouse they can provide an outstanding and colourful display for long periods. The variety 'Madame Butterfly' grows up to 1 m (3 ft) high and the double florets, if undamaged by wind or rain, are particularly striking. Each plant needs the support of a 1 m (3 ft) long cane and this is best inserted behind, but close to, the stem early in its life. Paper-covered wire ties put on as the stem grows will be inconspicuous at flowering time. Seeds are sown from January to March in heat and the plants moved in stages into 130 mm (5 in) pots to flower. They may be used also as cut flowers.

Many other garden annuals can be treated in a similar manner.

BEGONIA The fibrous-rooted begonias are half-hardy perennials best raised from seed and sown in heat from January to March. If sown thinly the more sturdy seedlings may be potted directly into 90 mm ($3\frac{1}{2}$ in) pots, in which they will flower. Those remaining can be pricked out into a seed tray, allowing no more than 32 per box, for summer bedding outdoors. Most varieties provide numerous flowers for long periods. Propagation is also possible by taking cuttings of young shoots in the spring from overwintered plants.

Right *Begonia semper florens* 'Flamingo' is one of the fibrous-rooted begonias which can be inexpensively raised from seed.

CALCEOLARIA The slipper flower seed is sown in June. The young plants do not like high temperatures and are best grown in a shaded frame in the summer months. House the plants just before the onset of the autumn frosts, for temperatures below freezing will kill them. If the frame is heated they may remain in it for several more weeks. A range of varieties is available and will provide colour for several months in later winter and early spring. The plants do not tolerate wet foliage, so avoid spraying overhead; neither do they like too much bright sunshine, and shading is sometimes necessary, The golden rule with *Calceolaria* is to grow cool, not hot.

Calceolarias provide a fine display in late winter and early spring.

CAPSICUM Often listed as the ornamental pepper, *Capsicum* is grown for the brilliant colour of its fruits rather than for its flowers. Sown at any time during the first six months of the year, when propagating space allows, the plants fruit best in 180 mm (7 in) pots. They need not occupy the greenhouse in the warm summer months, but if brought indoors before the frosts they will provide fruits through to Christmas as long as they are grown in cool rather than cold conditions.

CINERARIA These are available in a wide range of brilliant colours. They may be sown in pans or boxes in a cold frame from April to August. The early flowering 'Spring Glory' strain, sown in June, will flower within six months, and if successional sowings are made through to August successional flowering will continue through to April. The flowers last for eight weeks or more and the plants grow to a height of 200 to 250 mm (8 to 10 in). Aim to grow cool, but not in a cold greenhouse, in order to get compact foliage; high temperatures lead to soft, leggy growth.

FREESIA Although they may be grown in pots for display purposes, it is more usual to use freesias as cut flowers. In the former case grow them in 130 mm (5 in) pots; if you require cut flowers grow them in wooden boxes at least 130 mm (5 in) deep. They grow best in unheated or cool greenhouses and may be raised from seeds or corms. Seeds are sown from March to June in a potting compost and spaced no less than 25 mm (1 in) apart; they are not transplanted. They flower from autumn well into the winter months. After flowering, growth will continue for some time, but later, when foliage begins to die down, slowly reduce the amount of water and give up feeding altogether. The plants ultimately dry off and the corms which they have developed can be put aside for growing in future.

Freesias grown from corms will flower throughout the winter months in the greenhouse if the minimum temperature is above 10°C (51°F). August-planted corms normally flower about January; September/October-planted corms flower in February but need to be plunged after planting.

Above *Solanum*, the Christmas cherry. Daily syringing from flowering time encourages a good display of berries. **Right** *Freesia x kewensis* hybrids grow in a cool greenhouse and provide winter flowers.

IMPATIENS SULTANI The busy lizzie is an easy-to-grow plant that flowers perpetually through the summer. Many varieties are now available and the F_1 hybrids are greatly superior to earlier strains; the award-winning 'Imp' strain is especially worthy of note. *Impatiens* are best treated as half-hardy annuals; sown in heat in early spring, they will normally germinate in 14 to 21 days. Although usually grown as pot plants they also look well in mixed hanging baskets.

PRIMULA Many species of *Primula* provide a delightful show of colour during the winter months, although their seeds are unusually small and need to be carefully handled. Suitable species for the cool greenhouse include *P.* × *kewensis*, *P. obconica*, *P. malacoides* and *P. sinensis*. For winter flowering they are usually sown in May. *P. malacoides* (fairy primrose) is often preferred for spring flowering, in which case it should be sown in July. A word of warning: *P. obconica* may cause a rash to develop on people who handle the plant. Although you may not suffer in this way, you should think twice before giving examples of this attractive species to a friend.

SOLANUM CAPSICASTRUM The Christmas or winter cherry is a small, berry-bearing shrub ideal as a Christmas pot plant. Sown in heat in February, the seedlings are potted singly into 90 mm (3½ in) clay pots when large enough to handle. Unless they are one of the dwarfing varieties, pinch out the growing tips when the plants are 75 mm (3 in) high to encourage side shoots to develop. Provided the weather is not cold they may be transferred to a frame as early as May and are best plunged. They should be grown as cool as possible during the summer months. Syringing at least once a day, starting at flowering time and continuing during the summer, is recommended to obtain a good display of fruiting berries. Rehouse the plants in late September; they require temperatures of 7 to 10°C (45 to 51°F).

The following are brief notes on some additional flowering plants of more than ordinary interest that can be grown in the greenhouse:

ACHIMENES (MICHELSSEN HYBRIDS) Sow seeds in February/March. Flowers mid-summer to autumn. Repot in January.

BEGONIA X TUBERHYBRIDA The tuberous-rooted type, as opposed to fibrous-rooted forms (see above). Requires minimum temperature of 13°C (55°F). Start on damp peat in mid-March, and then pot. Summer flowers require shade. Overwinter tubers in a dry peat/sand mixture, preferably in the home.

CHLOROPHYTUM COMOSUM VARIEGATUM (SPIDER PLANT) Hardy pot plant with long, grass-like leaves with broad central white strip. Grows plantlets that are easily rooted. Repot annually.

COLEUS (FLAME-NETTLE) Valued for its bronze-red or deep pink leaves. Grow from seed. Remove any flowers that form. Propagate from cuttings.

FICUS ELASTICA 'ROBUSTA' The India-rubber plant makes fine specimen plants for the home. Needs a warm greenhouse, 13°C (55°F), and good but indirect sunlight. Do not overwater. Clean leaves regularly with proprietary leaf cleaner or mixture of 1 part milk to 2 parts water.

GERBERA JAMESONII (TRANSVAAL DAISY) Colourful perennial hybrids with large, daisy-shaped blooms. Sow seeds in February/March. Repot annually. Propagate vegetatively by side shoots.

SINNINGIA SPECIOSA (GLOXINIA) Perennial with fine, bell-shaped flowers and attractive dark-green leaves. Choose F_1 hybrid seeds and sow early in the year in warm greenhouse. Tubers may be kept from year to year; or propagate from leaf cuttings.

HEDERA HELIX (ENGLISH IVY) Many attractive varieties available. Grow in cool greenhouse as pot plant or in border, and allow to climb. Good for hanging baskets. Can eventually be planted outdoors.

Ficus elastica. The upper and lower surfaces of the leaves should be cleaned regularly. The varying leaf sizes of this example indicate that it has been fed irregularly.

KALANCHOË SPECIES Hardy winter-flowering plants with scarlet blooms, growing well in small pots. Perennial, though generally with poor flowers after first season. Sow seed in early spring; house plants in frames in summer. Some species develop plantlets on edges of leaves; others can be propagated by cuttings.

MIMOSA PUDICA (THE SENSITIVE PLANT) Its small, feather-like leaflets fold up tightly if touched, slowly re-opening. Grow as an annual from seed in the spring in warm greenhouse. Sow seeds in sandy compost.

PEPEROMIA CAPERATA Small, attractive pot plant with dark green, heart-shaped, crinkly leaves and white flowers. Propagate by leaf cuttings in warm greenhouse.

SAINTPAULIA (AFRICAN VIOLET) A worldwide favourite, with hundreds of varieties, flowering almost throughout the year in right conditions. Minimum temperature 16°C (60°F); but may be moved into cool greenhouse in summer; good light but with some shade from bright sun. Water moderately, with warm water. Propagate by leaf cuttings.

STEPHANOTIS FLORIBUNDA Vigorous evergreen climber with strongly scented tubular white flowers in summer and autumn. Propagate by cuttings of young wood. Prune heavily to restrict growth.

STREPTOCARPUS (TRIUMPH HYBRIDS) Colourful trumpet-shaped flowers of violet, blue, pink, red, or white in summer. Raise from seed in January in warm greenhouse. Flowers need warm conditions, shaded from bright sunlight.

TRADESCANTIA SPECIES Pot plants with colourful trailing foliage, different varieties having silvery, gold, pink, or purplish leaves. Propagate by cuttings; use about five rooted cuttings in each pot for best effect. Grow in warm greenhouse with good light.

Right above *Saintpaulia* make a fine display but need a minimum of 16°C (60°F). **Right below** January-sown *Streptocarpus* hybrids flower in late summer.

5 Food Crops

In recent years there has been renewed interest among amateur gardeners in growing salad and vegetable crops for the family, and, with the tendency for new gardens to be smaller than in the past, more intensive means of cultivation are finding favour. The traditional greenhouse has long been used for growing a range of salad crops, and with the advent of the less expensive polythene-covered structures, the range of food crops is being widened to include some popular cultivars hitherto grown mainly outdoors. Food crops grow just as well under polythene as they do under glass; indeed, many gardeners prefer the plastic-covered greenhouse for this type of plant. It is usual to grow food crops in the greenhouse border soil, and good light conditions at that level are important. The glass or polythene should extend down to soil level and be kept free of algae (the green film that inevitably builds up after a period of time). This growth can be particularly troublesome on the lower panes of glass, but it can easily be removed with a soft brush and soapy water.

Soil preparation

If it can be so arranged, you should rotate crops in the borders; for example, grow tomatoes in the east border in year one, in the west border in year two, and in the north border in year three. If the benching is fitted down one side only, move it to the other side every other year.

The preparation of the border soil is much the same for almost all food crops. It is important to appreciate that the border is a comparatively small area that is being intensively cultivated, so thorough preparation is essential. Dig the soil one spit deep (the depth of the blade of the spade). If the subsoil is compacted and therefore likely to impede drainage, break it up by forking, taking care not to bring subsoil to the surface, for roots go down a long way. Dig plenty of bulky organic matter such as rotted farmyard manure, compost, or peat into the topsoil. If the soil is very poor you should seriously consider replacing it, or working in John Innes potting compost, or even growing your crops in containers. The majority of plants do not like very acid soils and it may be necessary to add lime. The acidity/alkalinity level can be checked with an inexpensive soil *p*H testing kit; the optimum level for most greenhouse crops (including flowering plants) is slightly acid, a *p*H of 6.5.

During the course of a season the border subsoil tends to dry out to some extent and winter 'flooding' is an essential part of border preparation. Using a hosepipe fitted with a rose, a garden sprinkler with a fine spray, or other types of overhead irrigation, thoroughly soak the border, ensuring that the water gets down to the subsoil. Do this soon after digging is completed and allow several days for the surface soil to dry out before applying a base dressing of general fertilizer. This will need to be worked into the top few inches of soil at least three days before sowing or planting.

Growing methods

There is an increasing number of alternatives to growing in the border soil. Plants have been grown in pots since the early days, but as pot prices rise the polythene growing bag is becoming a popular and economic alternative. These sausage-shaped bags are bought ready filled with a complete compost and are well worth using if the border soil is poor or in need of sterilization or where it is advantageous to be able to move plants around.

Watering is a less simple operation than many people realise. If possible water should be applied in small droplets, and both the watering can and the hosepipe should be fitted with a rose; trickle irrigation is, of course, a suitable alternative. After the initial flooding, the aim should be to keep the soil moist, but not sodden, and to ensure that there are no dry patches. The grower with a glass-covered greenhouse also needs a syringe, which will deliver a fine, almost mist-like spray over the foliage during warm, sunny periods; this creates a good growing environment for the plants. The inexperienced gardener should ask a professional to demonstrate exactly what is required, or should visit the greenhouses of his local parks department. In polythene-covered structures constant high humidity may be a problem. It is caused by

To use all available space, pot-grown sweet peppers may be grown between tomato plants.

the beads of water which build up on the polythene sheet, and the remedy is less syringing of the plants.

The larger food plants need to be supported from early on in their life. Most can be loosely secured to a supporting cane. Alternatively, plants such as tomatoes can be supported by strings tied loosely to the plant just above soil level and secured at the other end to stout glazing bars or roof framework; as the plant grows the string is wrapped round the stem.

Clearing a crop when it is finished needs to be done carefully. At this stage of their life the plants may be infected with disease organisms both above and below soil level. They should therefore be cut down gently and loaded straight into a barrow. When forking out the roots, remove as much of the root growth as possible.

Tomatoes

Tomatoes are undoubtedly the most popular greenhouse crop and constitute the cornerstone of many greenhouse programmes. The flavour of freshly picked tomatoes is considered by most people to be better than that of fruits that have passed through wholesale and retail channels. In heated greenhouses tomatoes may be harvested from May to October; in unheated structures from August to October. The yield varies enormously, but it generally lies in the range of 3 to 7 kg ($6\frac{1}{2}$ to $15\frac{1}{2}$ lb) per plant, depending on whether the crop is grown without or with heat. A common mistake among amateurs is to grow too many tomatoes. If you find yourself with a surplus, consider deep freezing or, with the green fruits, making chutney. If tomatoes are grown in the same border year after year, yields will almost certainly decline markedly after the second crop owing to the build-up of diseases in the soil. Newcomers to tomato growing often obtain heavy crops in their first year only because the soil is free of such harmful organisms.

Left Preparing border soil: 1 After digging out one spit depth, break up subsoil; 2, 3 Replace topsoil, digging in plenty of organic matter; 4 Thoroughly soak the border.
Above Growing bags made of polythene do away with the need to sterilize border soil.

VARIETIES The choice is wide, with each variety having different points of merit. If you have a small greenhouse it is best to go for compact-growing plants which have their trusses close together. Varieties are available which are resistant to the disorder known as greenback, and first-cross hybrids may give heavier yields owing to their 'hybrid vigour'; a couple of recommended examples are 'Eurocross BB' for heated greenhouses and 'Alicante' for unheated ones. Grafted plants are available in some areas; the variety, raised in the usual manner, is grafted on to a form of wild rootstock when both are about the thickness of a pencil. The wild rootstock has some resistance to the more common soil diseases, and

'Gardeners Delight' tomatoes, with peppers.

consequently in some cases offers an alternative to soil sterilization.

PROPAGATION Temperatures of the order of 21°C (71°F) are needed in the early stages of propagation, and minimum day temperatures of 18°C (65°F) when the seedlings are potted. Temperatures as high as these are expensive to maintain in the early months of the year, and an alternative method is to buy in plants raised by a nurseryman. Although this reduces the satisfaction derived from raising one's own plants, it is better to do this than to propagate plants at lower temperatures than those recommended: conditions experienced by the plant early in its life affect the potential yield of the first three trusses.

If plants are raised from seed and early tomatoes are required, a late-November or early-December sowing is the rule for a heated crop. Sowing in heat in late February or early March will provide plants for a cold-house crop. Tomato propagation is straightforward: sow seeds thinly in boxes or pans; later, pot the seedlings into 90 mm ($3\frac{1}{2}$ in) pots, and finally plant from these into the border or containers.

CULTIVATION Where plants are to be grown in the border, thorough soil preparation, as described above, is essential because tomatoes are gross feeders. Planting in cold, wet soil will cause a major setback in growth, and it is preferable to transfer the plant to a bigger pot and stand it out on the border in its final position; planting can then take place when the soil conditions are more suitable. Plant 450 mm (18 in) apart: closer spacing greatly reduces air circulation, which can create growth problems. In narrow borders two rows may be grown if the plants are staggered. It is essential to ensure that the plants are not dry just before they are planted, and immediately after planting they should be watered in to settle the soil around them.

Tomatoes crop well in growing bags. The compost in these bags is scientifically formulated, with the correct plant foods already added. The bags warm up more quickly than the border soil, and consequently the plants get off to a good start. Bags can be put close together while the plants are small and placed in their final positions later – a valuable asset when greenhouse space is scarce in the spring. The roots of bag-grown tomatoes do not penetrate into the border soil and consequently do not contaminate it. Support the plants by stake or string soon after planting out.

The side shoots that grow in the leaf axils (where the leaf joins the stem) must be snapped out when small, and this is best done early in the day when the plants are turgid. The first trusses of early crops sometimes do not set, and the use of fruit-setting hormones is an invaluable aid.

The tomato plant needs moist atmospheric conditions for a short while each day to assist fruit setting, and this is best achieved by spraying over the plants with a syringe, preferably early in the day. You should water the plants by hand two or three times a week (daily if automatic irrigation is used), ensuring that sufficient water is supplied for the subsoil not to dry out. Healthy plants should not require shading; if they wilt in bright sunshine, look for another cause. Is the plant short of water? Has it a healthy root system? Tomatoes like a minimum night temperature of 12°C (54°F) and a minimum day temperature of 18°C (65°F); if automatic vents are fitted they should be set to open at 22°C (73°F). Regular liquid feeding of the plants throughout their period of growth is essential; a number of proprietary brands of feed is available.

The fruit, with the calyx attached, is best picked before it is fully ripe if the plant is heavily laden. Common fruit disorders are blossom-end rot and cracked fruit, which can both be attributed to deficiencies in watering.

Right above Tomato plants need to be supported by string (as here) or by a stake.
Right below Tomato side shoots should be removed when small. Do this early in the morning, when the plants are turgid.

Cucumbers

Cucumbers are widely grown under protective cover by amateur gardeners, and they will produce satisfactory crops in both heated and unheated structures. If grown well a couple of plants will provide the average family with an adequate supply of the fruit throughout the summer season. Cucumbers like very warm, moist conditions and for this reason do not grow well alongside many other food crops. If you wish to grow them with tomatoes you would be well advised to screen off a small area of the greenhouse with thin polythene so that the cucumber plants have a growing area all to themselves. In my experience cucumber plants grown in a polythene-covered greenhouse grow quite satisfactorily without such a screen, possibly because of the higher natural humidity. In fact, I favour growing them on their own in a garden frame, where I obtain results just as good as if they were in the greenhouse.

For best results cucumbers need to be grown on mounds of well-rotted horse manure or compost in very warm, moist conditions. To support the cucumbers, tie the stems with raffia to a cane or wire frame.

VARIETIES Most varieties of cucumbers produce male and female flowers and the male flowers have to be removed daily to ensure that the female flowers are not pollinated: if seeds are produced within the cucumber they give a bitter taste to the fruit. This time-consuming chore is now a thing of the past if varieties are chosen which produce only female flowers; 'Femspot' and 'Simex' are all-female F_1 hybrids highly recommended for growing in the greenhouse or frame. As with tomatoes, relatively high temperatures are required in the early stages of propagation and it may be preferable (and cheaper) to purchase plants from a nurseryman ready for immediate setting out. Buying in greenhouse plants needs rather more care than buying in bedding plants. In particular you should be satisfied that the plants have not been exposed to cold, windy conditions for any length of time; those that have spent several days outside an exposed shop front should be left well alone.

CULTIVATION Cucumber plants are very fussy about the soil in which they are cultivated. It is customary to prepare a raised bed, or mound, consisting mainly of fairly well-rotted, strawy horse manure if it is available; alternatively, you can use fairly well-rotted garden compost. In both cases the presence of partially decomposed plant material is an asset. Put a layer of good topsoil or potting compost on top of the bed and set the plants into this – provided the soil temperature is not too high. The decomposing matter will continue to generate some heat for a few weeks, which will encourage rapid growth of both roots and stem. The raised bed sinks with decomposition and should be topped up from time to time with more organic matter – although if the plants are grown in frames it may be impossible to do this without causing them damage.

Take care in supporting the plants in the greenhouse to avoid strangling them as the level of the rooting medium sinks. Supports may be of cane or wire, and in either case the plant should be secured to its support with raffia or paper-covered wire ties.

Cucumber plants like plenty of water and are gross feeders. They benefit from a weak plant-food solution at every watering. A high-nitrogen feed is best, because otherwise the plant will be starved of nitrogen as the organic matter in the bed decomposes. Allow the temperature in the greenhouse or frame to rise to 26°C (79°F) before opening the ventilators, and maintain a humid atmosphere by syringing the plants two or three times a day in hot weather; the greenhouse path should also be kept moist during the daytime. If the plant is growing well, shading should not be necessary.

Some training of the plant is essential. The main stem is allowed to grow naturally; the side shoots are trained to grow horizontally and on either side of the main stem. It is best to remove the lowest six laterals during the early stages of growth; the remainder are stopped after the second leaf has formed by pinching out the growing tip. Cucumbers are allowed to form on these lateral branches. As the season progresses the laterals may send out sub-laterals which should be stopped after the first leaf has formed; they will also bear fruit in turn. There are conflicting views as to whether it is wise to allow cucumbers to develop on the main stem; I myself allow all fruits that look healthy to develop.

Red spider mite is perhaps the most troublesome pest of this crop; if supporting canes are used, colonies of the mite tend to build up in them. This pest can be controlled by sprays or fumigants, but it should be noted that cucumber plants are harmed by sprays containing DDT.

When you clear the crop, spread what remains of the rotted compost over the border; it will enrich the soil and benefit subsequent crops. Some cost-conscious gardeners prefer to bag up the compost for use as a potting soil, but while it usually gives satisfactory results if used in this way it has drawbacks because the essential plant foods may be out of balance.

Lettuce

In recent years improvements in the rapid transport of food crops have been such that we have become accustomed to eating green salad plants such as lettuce throughout the year. In fact, the home greenhouse gardener can now provide lettuce for much of the year if he selects his varieties with care; in particular, fast-growing varieties raised in protected cultivation produce tender, succulent leaves. Relatively easy to grow, lettuce does exceptionally well under polythene and where soil-warming cables are used.

TYPES AND VARIETIES There are three main types: 'butter-heads', round-hearted lettuce with soft leaves; 'crisp-hearted', which have curled leaves; and 'cos', with straight upright leaves which form a loose heart. Many varieties are listed by seedsmen, and the two main factors that will determine your choice are whether the crop is to be grown cold, with gentle heat, or at fairly high temperatures, and the time of year of sowing and harvesting. The Glasshouse Crops Research Institute has raised a number of varieties that can be recommended; look also for varieties carrying the award of merit of the Royal Horticultural Society (AM, RHS). Make sure that the varieties selected are recommended for growing indoors.

PROPAGATION Seed may be sown directly into the border soil, as with outdoor lettuce, but this does not make for the best use of available space. It is better to sow in a seed tray and, as soon as the plants are big enough to handle, to move them to small peat pots. When doing this, handle the plant by a leaf and not by the stem, for the latter is very tender and easily bruised. Try to plant it at the same depth as it was in the seed tray, and settle the compost around it by lightly watering overhead.

CULTIVATION The plants will grow happily in these pots on shelving or benching for four to six weeks. They are then put out into the prepared border, spaced 230 to 300 mm (9 to 12 in) apart, depending on vigour of variety and type. Regular liquid feeding with a soluble plant food will help them to mature quickly. Lettuce like plenty of water and will succumb to a number of disorders if the growing medium dries out. When applying water, however, do so with care to avoid splashing soil on to the foliage. They also prefer alkaline soils to acid, and lime should be worked into the border as part of the preparatory work. Lettuce like good light conditions but not excessive heat. Ventilate the greenhouse in summer when temperatures rise above about 22°C (72°F). Slugs can be a problem, and the old gardener's remedy is to apply well-weathered soot to the soil surface just before planting; if this is not available use a slug bait. Botrytis, or grey mould, is the major disease, particularly of over-wintering lettuce in unheated conditions; greenfly is the most troublesome insect pest.

Left Three popular forms of lettuce: butter-head, crisp-hearted, and cos. Cos lettuces make quicker, tighter hearts if tied loosely with string or raffia just when hearting begins. **Below** Moving seedlings from the seed tray into their first pot. If this is carried out on the benching, it is advisable to use a polythene sheet to avoid spilling compost on to the bench gravel.

Courgettes

Courgettes, a type of small marrow, were once considered a gourmet's dish but are now widely grown for the family in the vegetable garden. They respond well to a little protection, producing numerous tender fruitlets from June through to October. When fully grown the plant can be as big as 1 m (3 ft) across, and as such is not suitable for the small greenhouse where space is at a premium. Courgettes are excellent for growing in the polythene greenhouse or in the garden frame.

VARIETIES The variety 'Green Bush' is my favourite. It is one of the earliest, has the Award of Merit of the RHS and the added vigour of an F_1 hybrid, and is recommended for freezing.

PROPAGATION Seeds may be sown in late March in the south of England and in mid-April in the north. Sow one seed per 90 mm (3½ in) pot filled with John Innes seed compost or a proprietary peat/sand mixture. A little heat is required; greenhouse border space can be saved by not planting out until such time as the roots almost fill the pot.

CULTIVATION Build a small mound of well-rotted compost on top of the prepared border soil and plant into this. Space plants at least 600 mm (2 ft) apart, planting in May if space allows. Plants surplus to requirements may be hardened off in the cold frame and planted outdoors when the danger of frost has passed. If the plant grows so vigorously that it seems to be getting out of hand, cutting the main stem back hard will check it without killing it. Courgettes will tolerate a wide range of temperatures, and consequently they fit in with many cropping programmes. As with almost all vegetable crops grown in protected cultivation, they welcome a syringing overhead on warm days. Grown well they are rarely troubled by pests; like other marrows, however, they are susceptible to virus diseases. It is essential to pick the fruits while they are small: 100 mm (4 in) is the ideal length.

Right above Courgettes grown under glass fruit long before those grown outside.
Right below Harvest the courgettes when they are about 100 mm (4 in) long.

Melons

Once looked upon as suitable only for the warmer greenhouse, melons can now be grown in unheated greenhouses, frames, and cloches on all but the coldest sites. This has been made possible by the work of the plant breeder. Few gardeners are likely to want to plant a greenhouseful of melons, but two or three plants worked into the summer cropping programme will produce a moderate harvest of fruits that will be welcome in the August to October period.

VARIETIES Selection of variety will depend upon whether the plants are to be grown with or without heat. In the former case choose from green–, white–, or scarlet-fleshed varieties; for colder conditions stick to the cantaloupe types such as 'Sweet-heart'.

PROPAGATION For the few plants that will be required it is best to sow one seed per 90 mm ($3\frac{1}{2}$ in) pot in April – the early part of the month for heated crops, the end of the month if the plants are to be grown on without heat. Propagating temperatures of around 21°C (71°F) are required initially; after the first pair of true leaves has formed, growth can continue at slightly lower temperatures. As soon as the roots begin to crowd the pot, the plants may be planted out in the border soil; if they are to be moved to cold frames or cloches, however, the plants will need first to be hardened off.

CULTIVATION Border preparation is similar to that described above for cucumbers; alternatively, plants may be grown in growing bags, and three plants will grow comfortably in each. Growing bags are especially suitable if you wish to grow melons on benching. In the greenhouse the plant will need support while it is still in its pot. Some training of the plant is essential: in frames and cloches pinch out the leader at the fifth leaf, and stop the lateral shoots that subsequently develop at the third leaf; in the greenhouse train the leader upwards.

Melons need to be pollinated by hand. Each female flower has a tiny fruit at its base. This is most easily pollinated by plucking off a male flower, removing its petals, and brushing the pollen into the female. Syringe the plants at least once a day. As fruits form, support those growing in the greenhouse with small nets and those in frames and cloches by placing a piece of slate or glass beneath each developing fruit. Start regular liquid feeding as soon as the first fruits form (earlier if the plants are being grown on organic mounds).

Pot-grown melons need training up canes from an early stage. The individual fruits may later need to be supported to prevent them breaking off their stem. The easiest way to do this is by tying them into string-net bags.

Sweet Peppers

Plant breeders have responded to the need for new varieties as the demand for peppers grows steadily year by year, and the recently introduced hybrids have performed well not only in greenhouses but also in cold frames. Two recommended varieties are 'Early Prolific' and 'New Ace'. Peppers grow exceptionally well in polythene-covered structures. Seeds are sown individually in small pots in March and propagated in temperatures similar to those maintained for tomatoes.

Well before the plants get potbound they should be moved into 130 mm (5 in) pots. Planting when the first flower bud is 2 to 3 mm (about $\frac{1}{8}$ in) in diameter gives the best results, and plants should be spaced 330 mm (13 in) apart in a single row, the site having been prepared well beforehand in the same way as for cucumbers. Frequent syringing on warm days will provide the humid conditions which help the fruit to set.

Peppers are normally harvested between July and October and should be picked when green if maximum yields are required. If left on the plant they will turn red, but in the process they will sap the plant's energy, and may reduce its potential yield by as much as one third.

Aphids can be a major pest of the crop; the main disease affecting sweet peppers is *Botrytis* (grey mould), which can often be prevented or reduced in effect if the plant and its surroundings are kept as clean as possible.

Left Pot-grown peppers are normally picked green in mid-summer to early autumn. Allowing them to remain on the plant until they have turned red will considerably reduce the potential yield of each plant. **Right** Salad crops grow especially rapidly under polythene-covered structures and are consequently tender and tasty. Varieties of many salad crops have been bred especially for intensive cultivation, allowing two crops per season to be grown.

Beetroots, Carrots, Turnips, and Radishes

Provided suitable varieties are chosen – take your seedsman's advice on this – these crops, more usually grown out of doors, can all be cultivated under glass or in polythene-covered greenhouses. Under these conditions the more rapid growth that results means more tender vegetables and, in warmer regions at least, the possibility of two crops per season instead of one.

Varieties of all these crops have been bred specially for intensive cultivation of this nature, and their most noticeable feature is their compact foliage. Root-crops like rich but not freshly manured soil, and the seed may be thinly broadcast on the border and lightly raked in rather than being sown in drills as is usual outdoors.

Partly protected plants

The food crops discussed above are from plants that spend most if not all their lives under glass or polythene. Below are some plants that are grown mainly outdoors but can be brought into the greenhouse for forcing or other purposes. This is an interesting and important secondary role for the greenhouse, but it should not be allowed to interfere with your prime-purpose cropping regime.

Rhubarb

'Timperley Early' is one of the earliest varieties of outdoor rhubarb. It can be forced early in the year in the greenhouse with little difficulty as long as space is available to provide the rather special conditions the plant requires.

The plants are grown in the open ground in the usual manner and provided with a plentiful supply of well-rotted organic matter during the growing season. Apply this to the soil surface and allow worm activity to incorporate it in the soil. Pulling of rhubarb sticks from plants that are to be forced the following winter should stop early in the season to ensure big, plump crowns.

In November the selected crowns, which should be at least two years old, must be exposed to frost to bring on their brief dormant period. Soon after Christmas carefully dig up the crowns and move them to the greenhouse, where they should be replanted in a dark place – beneath the staging, for instance. Water them well to settle the soil around them. Depending on the amount of heat available, the buds will soon start into growth; they should not be exposed to light except for picking, and the sticks are pulled when they are about 250 mm (10 in) long.

Slugs may be troublesome and slug bait should be put out as a preventive measure. After cropping the crowns are best thrown away, as this forcing treatment exhausts them.

Rhubarb being forced in the dark beneath a greenhouse bench. Crowns of outdoor varieties selected for forcing should be brought in from the kitchen garden and planted in the border soil in the last days of December.

Peas

Many people still prefer fresh garden peas to tinned or frozen ones, and winter sowings outdoors of the hardy round-seeded varieties will allow picking to start in early June. The wrinkle-seeded peas are less hardy and consequently a little later but their flavour is markedly better. The greenhouse owner can, with a little effort and expertise, get wrinkle-seeded peas podding early by growing them in their initial stages under glass or polythene. Two varieties suitable for this treatment are 'Early Onward' and 'Kelvedon Wonder', neither of which need be staked. They can be sown six to eight weeks earlier than would be normal outdoors. The first thing to be done is to make rectangular troughs from thin planks of wood which have been treated with wood preservative (but on no account use creosote). The troughs should have interior dimensions of about 1 m by 150 mm (3 ft by 6 in) and should be about 150 mm in depth; a 150 mm (6 in) wide plank forms the bottom of the trough and is kept in place by string. Fill the troughs with improved garden soil or, better still, with spent cucumber compost. Sow the seeds somewhat thicker than is normal – that is, two rows with seeds 50 mm (2 in) apart and at a depth of about 75 mm (3 in). In the protected conditions germination is usually speedy and the troughs can be transferred to a garden frame when pressure on greenhouse space builds up.

After hardening off, and not before April in the south and May in the north, take the troughs to the planting site. Dig out a suitable trench and put the troughs into it. Cut the strings retaining the bottom plank and carefully remove the trough and plank. Rake the soil around the newly planted row to settle the plants; they should now grow satisfactorily having suffered no root disturbance. This system of growing can be adapted to other crops if space allows.

Early pickings of peas may be obtained by sowing seeds in troughs which have removable bottom boards. Raised in heat, the young plants, still in the trough, are hardened off before they are planted out.

Runner Beans

The earliest pickings of outdoor runner beans come from plants raised with some protection and grown as ground beans – that is, plants unsupported by canes and from which the growing tip was pinched when the plant was about 300 mm (12 in) tall. Sowings are made in April under cloches, spacing the individual seeds 150 mm (6 in) apart in the row and later thinning to 250 mm (10 in). The soil should have been well manured during the winter months. Alternatively the young plants may be put out as soon as any danger of frost has passed. About one month before the anticipated planting date fill large, shallow boxes with an already used compost mixed with peat to a depth of 100 mm (4 in). Sow the beans 75 mm (3 in) apart and place the boxes in a warm greenhouse at about 12°C (54°F). As soon as most of the seedlings have emerged, remove the boxes to the garden frame and give the plants protection with a sheet of newspaper on nights when frost is forecast. The plants need to be properly hardened off. When it comes to planting time, prise the plants carefully out of the growing boxes, keeping as much root intact as possible, and plant them 250 mm (10 in) apart in the row. In dry weather it will help them to become established if you spray them lightly for the first few days with a watering can fitted with a fine rose.

Strawberries

The earliest home-grown strawberries are produced under glass from maiden (one-year-old) plants. Until recently they were often grown singly in 130 mm (5 in) pots, but it is now more fashionable to grow them in purpose-made wooden barrels or strawberry urns, which may have an overall height of more than 1 m (3 ft). An alternative, more suitable for the smaller greenhouse, is to grow them in a horizontal plastic pipe, about 100 mm (4 in) in diameter, which is hung from the glazing bars in place of shelving. When grown within the protection of a greenhouse, strawberries are available several weeks earlier than those grown outdoors. They can be followed by strawberries pot-grown in a frame, while strawberries grown in the soil under cloches still fruit well in advance of those without any protection.

Strawberry plants rapidly degenerate with virus disease and it is best to buy pot-grown plants which have a certificate of health and have been raised by a specialist grower. Varieties such as 'Cambridge Favourite' give the earliest fruit, and August planting will enable them to establish themselves rapidly. Fill the containers with a potting compost, and provide them with good drainage. The planted containers remain out of doors until February. When brought into a cool greenhouse the plants quickly break into growth and will need regular feeding with a high-potash feed from then onwards. Keep an eye out for slugs and snails as well as aphids. Allow air to circulate freely around the containers, and remove runners as they appear. After they have fruited move the plants outside, trim back the foliage lightly with shears, and retain for fruiting one more year only.

'Cambridge Favourite' strawberries growing in disused guttering in John Innes compost.

Vines

These are still widely grown under glass, and with careful attention will produce many bunches of grapes a year. However, their heavy canopy of summer leaf cuts out a great deal of light in the greenhouse, and few crops will grow satisfactorily beneath them at that time of year. Moreover, in the dormant winter period they prefer really cold conditions, so ventilators need to be left open – conditions which most other greenhouse plants will not tolerate. Vines are best planted in border soil just *outside* the greenhouse, and the main stem taken inside through a hole in the wall.

With the increasing interest in growing grapes, specialist raisers are offering a wider range of varieties, but the older 'Black Hamburgh' remains one of the best. Young pot-grown vines are normally planted in the winter months, and the border soil should be enriched with loam and manure. Little or no fruit can be expected until three years after planting. The rods (main stems), of which there may be one or two, and the lateral growths are secured by soft string to rows of supporting wires fixed some 250 mm (10 in) below the roof of the greenhouse. Annual winter pruning consists of cutting back the lateral growths to the main stem. Vines can bleed profusely, so they should be fully dormant when this operation is carried out. The bunches of grapes are thinned with special vine scissors, the object being to shape the bunch and remove small, immature fruits that could become mildewed; an old umbrella hung upside down from the wires while you do this job will catch the small fruits and allow their easy removal from the greenhouse.

A well-trained young vine. Regular tying-in is necessary. Vines grow rapidly, and the lateral growths need to be cut back to the main stem every winter. After the second season's growth, cut the main stem back to about 1.5 m (5 ft) of new wood.

6 Plant Propagation

PLANT propagation is an activity that most greenhouse owners find rewarding and to which, ultimately, they devote much time. Attention to detail is what distinguishes the successful from the less successful in this field. Even the most adept gardener is likely to fail unless he maintains the highest standards of hygiene in the greenhouse, for seeds and young plants are very susceptible to a variety of diseases. Propagation usually requires heating to temperatures above the 'cool' greenhouse level of 7°C (45°F). This can, of course, be localized (so saving heating bills) if you have a propagating case, which you can either buy or make yourself.

Special composts are available for propagating purposes. In the John Innes range the seed compost is less coarse than the potting mixtures, while cutting composts usually contain a greater proportion of sand to improve soil aeration. In addition, there is a number of proprietary cutting composts which in themselves have little or no food value but provide ideal conditions for root initiation. It is important to realize that the environment in which a plant is propagated can affect its performance not only during the first few weeks and months but throughout its life. For example, lettuce plants raised with supplementary lighting during the winter months will ultimately develop lettuces with more leaves per plant than those raised at ordinary light levels; and tomato plants that were raised at temperatures somewhat lower than the optimum 20°C (69°F) commonly have a smaller yield on the first three trusses.

Propagation by seed

Propagation by seed is an inexpensive way to raise many types of greenhouse plants, although in the case of slower-growing species it may take much longer to obtain a worthwhile specimen. Generally, individual plants raised from seed are not identical to

their parents nor to one another, but such variation is often scarcely noticeable because, over a period of years, seed raisers select the 'truest' strains. You will find that catalogues from reputable seedsmen contain more and more seeds that are offered as F_1 hybrids – that is, the first-generation seed offspring of two pure-bred strains. Although they are more expensive (because they are the result of pollination by hand), they produce more vigorous, healthier plants. As a general principle, always ensure that any seed you buy is fresh, and try to synchronize your seed-buying and seed-growing activities.

There is less chance of transmitting disease from one generation to the next when seed is used, and although there are seed-borne diseases many seedsmen treat the seed before sale to prevent any such diseases from spreading. Different species of seeds vary enormously in the time they take to germinate. A guide to germination periods is given in many seed catalogues, and it is a good idea to take note of these periods so that you can use the propagating space in your greenhouse to greatest advantage. It is best to use a seed pan if only a few plants are required and to use a seed tray 50 mm (2 in) deep for larger quantities. Do not sow too thickly, for crowded seedlings tend to damp off. Some gardeners use a thin metal template with holes drilled in it, placing it over their seed trays to indicate correct spacing. Templates of 8 holes by 5 holes (40 seeds), 9 holes by 7 holes (63 seeds) and 10 holes by 8 holes (80 seeds) are useful. Sowing at stations in this manner may save prick-

Above left Seed sowing: a box of this size will take 250 seeds at most. **Right** A propagating case heated by low-voltage cables. In the foreground is a capillary watering unit.

Propagation by seed: after sowing, cover seeds thinly with compost; then cover tray with sheets of polythene and brown paper.

ing out. After sowing, the seeds should be covered by a thin layer of compost. This is firmed with a presser. The pan or box is next watered, preferably by standing it in a tray of water 20 mm ($\frac{3}{4}$ in) deep for about 30 minutes. It is then removed and covered with a sheet of glass or polythene and a piece of brown paper to exclude the light.

The covering materials should be removed as soon as the majority of seeds have germinated; from now on the seedlings must have good light conditions or spindly plants will result. However, many seedlings will tolerate a slightly lower temperature from this stage onwards.

In the case of seedlings such as bedding plants which are ultimately to be planted in open ground, it is important to make sure that they are prepared for the move from the warmth and protection of the greenhouse to outdoor conditions. This is the conditioning process known as hardening off, and it involves moving the plants to a closed frame, and then increasing the amount of ventilation they receive on warm, sunny days until the frame top is left off altogether – at first during daylight hours and eventually around the clock. Do not forget to provide weak liquid feeds at this time, for competition in seed trays can be severe. Although it is common to see bedding plants on sale that are already in flower, it is not desirable to let them reach this stage before planting out.

Stem cuttings: 1 Remove bottom leaves from cuttings; 2 Plant cuttings around edge of a pot filled with a cutting compost; 3 Place pot in a heated propagating frame.

Vegetative propagation

This is a form of propagation in which pieces of a plant are removed and rooted in the soil. Unlike plants raised from seed, those resulting from vegetative propagation are identical to their parents. Plants from which material is taken need to be carefully selected, for if there is disease (such as a virus) present it will automatically be transmitted. On occasions plants undergo a physiological change known as 'sporting'. A white chrysanthemum may sport yellow flowers, and yellow varieties sport deeper yellow or even red flowers. If shoots carrying such blooms are vegetatively propagated by means of layering (see below), a new variety will have come into being.

The following are the more common forms of vegetative propagation.

STEM CUTTINGS These may be of softwood or hardwood. The former are taken when the plant is actively growing and the latter are taken when it is dormant during the winter months. Many greenhouse plants may be propagated by means of softwood cuttings taken in the spring, typical examples being carnations, chrysanthemums, fuchsias, hydrangeas, and pelargoniums; in the case of pelargoniums stem cuttings are also taken in August.

Parent plants should be selected with care and be true to type. They must be vigorous and healthy and show no symptoms of attack by pests or diseases. The cuttings should be removed with a razor blade or very sharp knife. Select a non-flowering shoot 75 to 100 mm (3 to 4 in) long and make a cut 3 mm ($\frac{1}{8}$ in) above a node (leaf joint). If you cut at this point the chance of die-back will be reduced; long cuttings are of no advantage. The cutting is prepared by removing the bottom two or three leaves and making a clean cut just below a node. Check again that no aphids or red spider mites are present; if they are, immerse the cutting in a weak insecticidal solution. A rooting hormone may be used to assist propagation.

Insert the cuttings around the edge of a 130 mm (5 in) clay pot or pan filled with a cutting compost. Use a blunt dibber to make the holes, and the fingers to firm the compost after insertion. A propagating frame, preferably with bottom heat and an air temperature of 18 to 21°C (65 to 70°F), will help the cuttings to root quickly. Alternatively, the cuttings may be rooted on a sunny window sill in the home by inserting four small split canes 250 mm (10 in) long around the pot and placing it in a polythene bag. Rooted cuttings should be potted on as soon as possible because cutting composts are usually low on fertilizers.

LEAF CUTTINGS *Begonia rex*, in its innumerable varieties, and *Saintpaulia* (African violet) are typical examples of pot plants that can be propagated by leaf cuttings. In the case of *B. rex* the whole leaf is normally used. On the reverse side of the leaf, cut through the veins with a razor blade in several places, and then put the leaf right way up on a pan filled with cutting compost topped up with a thin layer of fine sand. Use small hoops of wire to peg down the leaf so as to ensure good contact with the compost, and then place the pan in a warm propagating frame. Young plants develop at the incisions in the leaf veins.

With *Saintpaulia*, strong young leaves are selected and each leaf blade together with the leaf stem is inserted individually in a small pot. After a while a cluster of small leaves will develop and the new plant may be potted-on.

AIR LAYERING This method of propagation is used on the taller pot plants if they become 'leggy' or look out of proportion owing to the loss of their lower leaves. Layering has the advantage that the plant remains intact while a new root system is being formed; it is best done in the spring and summer months. Two upward-sloping incisions about 40 mm ($1\frac{1}{2}$ in) long are made into opposite sides of the less woody part of the stem. The cuts are dusted with root-promoting hormones and a wad of damp sphagnum moss about the size of a tennis ball is put around the cut area. On top of this a sheet of thin polythene film is secured and lightly bound round the top and bottom to prevent the escape of mois-

Air layering *Ficus elastica*: 1 Make upward-sloping cuts in stem and dust them with a hormone rooting powder; 2 Enclose cuts in a piece of clear polythene filled with dampened sphagnum moss; 3 Secure polythene above and below cuts; 4 When new roots have formed in the cuts, sever the stem below them, remove the polythene and moss, and pot the new plant.

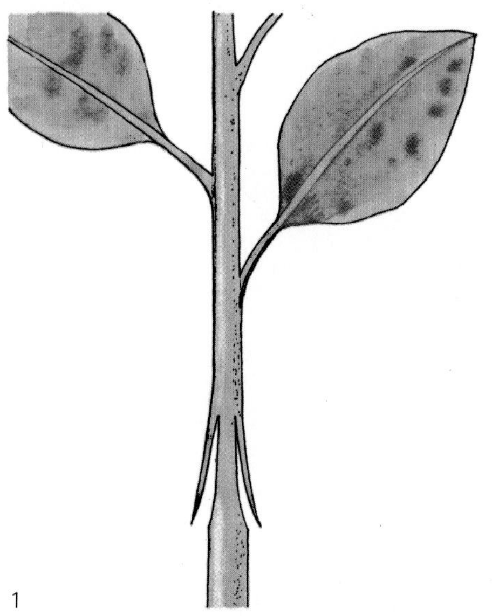
1

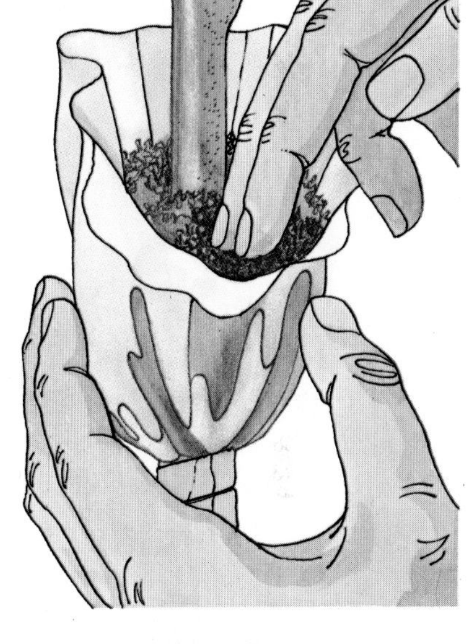
2

3

4

ture. Roots will develop over a period of months, and when they can be seen through the polythene the newly rooted plant should be severed from the parent and potted.

GRAFTING This method is rarely used to propagate greenhouse plants, with the occasional exception of tomatoes. But since tomato growing is an important feature of most home greenhouses, the method used for these plants deserves to be mentioned here. The value of tomato grafting is that it enables the grower to graft selected varieties on to rootstocks that have been bred specifically to resist various common root disorders. Seeds of the rootstock are sown 7 to 10 days before those of the variety; the seeds of both should be well spaced out in their trays, 36 seeds per tray being about right.

Grafting should be done when the seedlings of both variety and rootstock are about the thickness of a pencil. An upward-sloping incision about 30 mm ($1\frac{1}{2}$ in) long is made in the stem of the variety, while an identical but downward-sloping incision is made in the rootstock stem. Then the 'tongue' formed by the incision in the variety stem is slipped into the incision in the rootstock, and the union is bound with adhesive tape. The rootstock is now potted, and the entire plant is placed in a polythene tent for three or four days to reduce loss of moisture through the leaves. The tape is removed as soon as variety and rootstock are effectively growing as one plant. The portion of rootstock stem above the point of union can be removed in due course.

Grafting selected tomato variety to a rootstock: 1 Make incisions in variety and rootstock stems; 2 Bind the union with adhesive tape; 3 Pot the rootstock; 4 Enclose plant in polythene tent.

Propagating equipment

I have explained that the conditions under which a new plant is raised can have a bearing on its long-term growth. For this reason you will find that good propagation equipment is a worthwhile investment.

Plants generally need a uniformly warm temperature during this period and prefer the heat to come from the bottom rather than from the top (whence the term 'bottom heat'). In the case of cuttings it is essential to reduce moisture loss from the leaves, and high air humidity in the immediate vicinity is the best way of achieving this. Seedlings and cuttings also require sunlight if they are to develop normally, and the once-common practice of covering cuttings with newspaper is today frowned upon by progressive gardeners.

All these conditions can be achieved by the use of a propagating frame. Its size will depend on the amount of space available, and some simple calculations will be necessary to work out how many plants are likely to be at the propagating stage at peak times in the spring.

There are numerous makes of plant-propagating units. The bottom heat usually comes from thermostatically controlled warming cables or plates of 40 to 75 watts output, so running costs will amount to only a few pence per week. The covers for these units may be of light-gauge polythene sheeting, of rigid plastic, or of glass; sufficient height is required to allow the inclusion of small plants in pots. Some designs are bigger and more robust, in effect providing small greenhouses within the greenhouse. Most such models provide air heating as well as bottom heating by means of warming cables running around the interior walls; they enable relatively big plants to be housed within and can prove a great fuel saver to the enthusiastic amateur who does not want to heat the whole greenhouse.

It is essential to use purpose-made electrical connectors for all plant propagators, otherwise the moisture associated with propagation is likely to cause short-circuiting and consequent power failure.

Mist Propagation

Mist propagation units automatically provide cuttings with the optimum conditions for rooting by keeping moisture on the leaves at all times; this prevents cuttings from wilting. The unit is open to allow maximum light to reach the plants. In addition to these advantages, the cuttings are less susceptible to disease.

Propagation units of this type consist of one or more mist nozzles, a detector which indicates when the leaves are almost dry, a solenoid valve to switch the water supply on and off automatically, and a filter. Most units have built-in or separate soil-warming equipment. Cuttings are inserted in the normal way, and will develop roots more quickly in these units than in a less sophisticated propagating case. Once rooted, the plants require some form of 'weaning', and the more expensive mist propagators can be adjusted for less frequent misting. This drier regime normally continues for a few days, after which the plants are removed from the unit. The automatic system is designed to prevent the compost from becoming too wet; nevertheless the compost should be of a free-draining type. Soil temperatures of 21 to 24°C (71 to 77°F) are recommended. Incidentally, many amateur gardeners use such equipment for keeping established pot plants adequately watered during their absence, for instance over long weekends in the summer.

Artificial lighting

I have stressed the importance of good light conditions on a number of occasions, and the greenhouse owner whose growing programme relies on a busy propagating period early in the year would do well to consider seriously some system of providing supplementary lighting. At this time of relatively short days a period of dull weather can cause quite a setback to plants being propagated, and supplementary lighting will overcome this problem. Although expensive sodium or mercury lamps are used in commercial greenhouses, the amateur will find warm white or white fluorescent tubes quite satisfactory if they are suspended 450 to 600 mm (18 to 24 in) above the seedlings in the propagating area. This additional light calls for higher temperatures – of the order of 16°C (62°F) – in the vicinity of the plants, but some of the additional heat will be provided by the lights themselves.

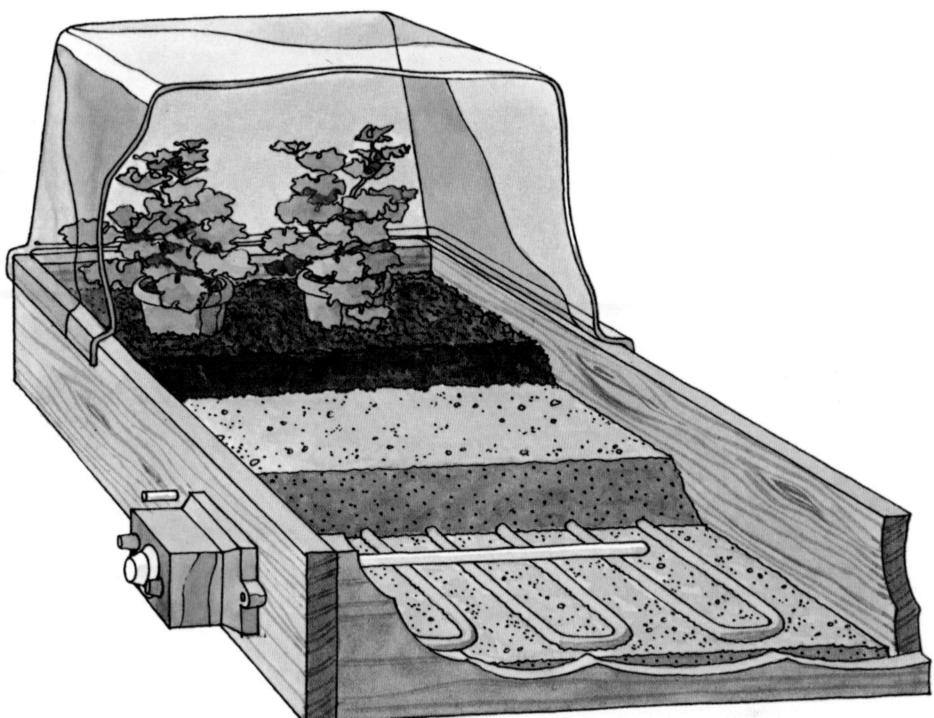

Above A propagating frame. The soil-warming cables are buried in sand underlying a layer of compost. **Below** Mist units keep the leaves of cuttings moist. Some propagating frames include automatically metered mist units.

7 Keeping Plants Healthy

This chapter could have been titled 'controlling pests and diseases', but that would have misrepresented its essential aim. There can be little doubt that every greenhouse gardener, whether amateur or professional, has at one time or another had to deal with plants that have been attacked by pests or infected by disease. Equally, every experienced gardener will tell you that prevention is better than cure, and that the most effective method of keeping pests and diseases at bay is to ensure that your plants are fundamentally healthy and that they are growing in a hygienic environment.

The truth of this is reflected in the fact that the good gardener seems to use far fewer insecticides and fungicides than the inexperienced amateur. His advantage lies not so much in his use of superior plant varieties as in his knowledge of plants and their idiosyncrasies and in his ability to recognize at an early stage the tell-tale signs of trouble. Every plant in the greenhouse needs to be examined thoroughly and often, and the shrivelled leaf, the weakly side shoot, the broken stem, and other sources of potential trouble removed. In the long run this work can be just as important as examining plants for the more obvious warning signs – the presence of a solitary snail or insect, or the smallest patch of mildew.

Here, then, are some obvious (and a few not so obvious) hints on growing healthy plants:

- Start with clean plant material: carefully examine any plant or cutting that is to be introduced into the greenhouse from another source. If it shows the slightest sign of disease or is carrying insect pests, these must be dealt with before it is allowed into the greenhouse.
- Keep newly introduced plants isolated from the others for about a fortnight if possible. Polythene is an aid to this, but alternatives are a frame or large empty propagating case.
- Buy new plants from a reliable nurseryman; he has a reputation to uphold and will not wish to sell you plants with problems.
- When propagating vegetatively use only material taken from first-class, selected plants.
- If you are a smoker, always wash your hands before handling tomato plants; some virus diseases of tobacco can be transmitted by hand.
- Sterilize all used plant pots and boxes with a weak solution of formaldehyde (not forgetting the crocks that go in the pots). Do this outside, and allow the containers to dry before returning them to the greenhouse.
- Know your enemies: learn to identify all the common greenhouse pests and diseases at an early stage.
- Use sterilized seed and potting composts. If a compost is being re-used do not grow the same species in it.
- Have a 'clean' area in the greenhouse where clean pots, boxes, and potting materials cannot become contaminated. Always brush down the potting bench after use.
- Rotate crops in the border soil whenever possible. After a crop such as tomatoes has been grown for two consecutive years in the same border soil, the yield per plant falls dramatically owing to the build-up of soil diseases.
- When growing plants in containers on contaminated border soil, isolate the border with polythene sheeting; white polythene with a black reverse side is ideal, for it will reflect light and thus assist plant growth.
- Pests and diseases often develop under paths: construct paths of removable paving stones.
- Avoid bringing soil into the greenhouse on boots and garden tools – it may contain harmful organisms that will spread diseases.
- Avoid handling diseased and clean plants at the same time. Virus diseases are, in fact, spread in many ways, but hands and knives are common carriers.
- When moving plants from seed tray to pot, or when potting on, plant at the same depth as before.
- Always handle seedlings by their leaves, not by their stems. Grip the leaf blade lightly between thumb and first finger. Very small seedlings are best handled with a match-like stick with a V notch cut in one end.
- Take prompt action to stop water drips in greenhouses. Excessive moisture not only locally waterlogs compost or border soils but may assist the spread of disease.
- Ensure that plants are fed regularly during periods of active growth.
- Give the inside and outside of the greenhouse a thorough clean at least once a year.

The shaped lance of this pump-up sprayer helps to get the diluted spray material on to all parts of the plants, especially the undersides of leaves.

Even if these and other measures are taken, however, you are virtually certain to have sickly plants on your hands at some time or other. The sources of trouble can be divided into four categories: pests, diseases, physiological disorders, and deficiencies. I have listed the most common of them below, with suggestions for action. When recommending chemical control, I have omitted mentioning specific chemicals, but I have listed some of the main proprietary products on pages 86–7. Note that certain chemicals, although effective against a given pest, may also harm some plant species. Most garden shops and horticultural stores can provide manufacturers' charts that indicate species, dosage rates, and frequencies recommended for treatment of plant disorders by particular products.

Pests

APHIDS Greenfly and blackfly are among the most common of the greenhouse insect pests. They normally cluster together and are easily seen with the naked eye. Aphids are sap suckers and if present in large numbers their feeding soon checks the plant's growth; they are also major carriers of virus diseases. They can be controlled with a variety of chemicals.

EARWIGS These are likely to damage open flowers by eating the petals; they are particularly active at night. The hollow ends of garden canes are common hiding places, and earwigs can be successfully controlled by trapping. Several small pots, half filled with wood wool, should be inverted over garden canes within the greenhouse or frame. The earwigs hide in the wood wool and are then easily shaken from it and killed.

LEAF MINER The maggot of the leaf miner tunnels between the upper and lower layers of the leaf before it pupates; this results in unsightly foliage. If no action is taken the fly that emerges from the pupa stage will lay more eggs. If only a few leaves are affected remove them by hand and burn them. Otherwise control them with a suitable insecticidal spray, repeating this treatment twice at fortnightly intervals.

RED SPIDER MITES These are sap suckers and attack plants from the underside of the leaves. The very small red mites are usually visible because of their delicate webs and their large numbers. The sucking causes the leaf to become mottled and then yellow. Spraying needs to be very thorough and directed particularly at the underside of the leaf; for this reason fumigants are preferred by many gardeners. The possibility of further infestation can be reduced by increasing greenhouse humidity.

Leaf miner attack is easily recognised. Remove affected leaves by hand and burn.

Below left Blackfly on runner beans. Such colonies build up rapidly and severely check the growth of plants. **Below** Sap-sucking aphids on a cyclamen plant.

Red-spider mites cause a characteristic bronzing of the upper leaf surfaces.

SCALE INSECTS Troublesome pests, scale insects are a particular nuisance on leaves and stems of house plants. The brown soft scale is the most common and is about 3 mm ($\frac{1}{8}$ in) long. The adults do not move and infestation often begins on the underside of the leaves. If only small numbers are present they may be removed with cotton wool dipped in methylated spirits. Alternatively use a systemic insecticide, a type that is absorbed by a plant through its leaves or from the soil and spreads throughout the plant's tissues.

SLUGS AND SNAILS These common garden pests relish some species of seedlings and young plants, and breed wherever rubbish is left lying around. Clean greenhouses and cold frames get few intruders. Slug baits are effective if kept dry, and if you have overwintering lettuce they should be used as a routine measure.

WHITEFLY A pest of many plants under glass. The adult flies, about 1 mm ($\frac{1}{25}$ in) long, normally inhabit the topmost leaves and rise into the air when the plants are disturbed. The larvae suck sap and excrete a honeydew on to fruit and foliage, and this encourages the growth of a dark sooty mould. Fumigants are usually the best means of control, but if they fail to achieve good results the introduction of the parasite *Encarsia formosa* should be considered (see below).

Whitefly: the flies are seen here with examples of the pupal stage.

Diseases

BOTRYTIS CINEREA Commonly known as grey-mould disease, *Botrytis* is a fungus that attacks a wide range of plants, particularly in cold, wet spells. It usually gains entry through damaged plant tissues, and it is a particularly troublesome source of damage to overwintered crops in unheated and cool greenhouses. As its name suggests it develops a fluffy grey mould on the infected plants. It is best prevented by keeping the foliage and stems of plants dry when the temperature is low and keeping air on the move. Fan heaters are good aids to *Botrytis* control, as are sprays of certain systemic fungicides, which are absorbed by the plants' tissues and protect against disease.

VIRUS DISEASES Often very difficult to detect, especially in their early stages, virus diseases may cause poor growth of plants, distorted foliage and flowers, pale and dark areas on the leaves, and stunting. They are spread in a number of ways, the most common being through root contact, through sap-sucking insects such as aphids, or by means of the hands or of cutting and pruning implements. It is essential to start with clean stock and propagate only from strong healthy plants. There

Botrytis cinerea, or grey-mould disease, on tomato plant foliage.

are no known means of cure available to the amateur gardener, and any plant considered suspect should be isolated and removed for burning. An exception to this is the tomato plant, which is prone to a virus disease when at about the third truss stage; with careful tending, however, tomato plants should survive this disease and go on to produce a reasonable crop.

TOMATO LEAF MOULD This is specific to tomatoes and is widespread. The symptoms are blotchy yellowing of the leaf surface in the early stages, followed by shrivelling and death. The disease is caused by stagnant, damp conditions brought about by insufficient movement of air in the greenhouse, and it can be particularly troublesome in polythene structures. Ensure movement of air overnight by leaving the vents open slightly during the summer months; this should prevent any steaming up of the greenhouse interior.

ROOT DISEASES Plants need a healthy, vigorous root system for optimum growth. Container-grown plants growing in modern composts rarely have root problems, and when they do it is usually caused by too much or too little water. On the other hand plants such as cucumbers and tomatoes grown in the same border soil year after year frequently have root problems caused by one or more of a number of root diseases. Affected plants wilt in periods of hot sun and most will ultimately die; curing them is difficult, if not impossible. Preventive measures include rotating crops in the borders, moving the greenhouse to a fresh site (often possible with polythene greenhouses), soil changing, and soil sterilization. If none of these alternatives is possible, you would be well advised to grow your tomatoes and cucumbers in polythene growing bags.

DAMPING OFF A disease that occurs frequently among seedlings in pans and trays, causing them to collapse at the base of the stem. It may be prevented by using a sterilized compost and sterilized containers, by the use of appropriate fungicidal seed dressings, and by using the copper-based Cheshunt compound fungicide, watered on soon after germination and when transplanting seedlings.

Tomato leaf mould, caused by overcrowding.

Physiological disorders

Tomatoes suffer from a number of such disorders. 'Greenback' is the name given to fruits which, when ripe, still have green or yellow patches on them. It is a less common disorder than formerly owing to the introduction of resistant varieties. Cracked fruits occur as a result of a sudden upsurge of moisture into the plant; this often happens after soil which has been allowed to become too dry receives a good soaking of water. The cracks, however, may not appear until some time later.

Cucumbers and courgettes provide examples of fruiting plants in which the developing fruitlet occasionally turns yellow and prematurely dies. The reason for this is often difficult to determine, as it can be caused by a variety of factors. The plant may be under some strain; it may, for instance, already be carrying many fruits, or the feeding may be at fault – in which case high-potash feeds could be beneficial. Low temperatures can upset plant growth, particularly if they coincide with several dull days with little or no sunshine. Developing fruitlets which have such disorders should be carefully cut from the plant with a sharp knife and removed from the greenhouse or frame.

Damping-off disease of pea seedlings.

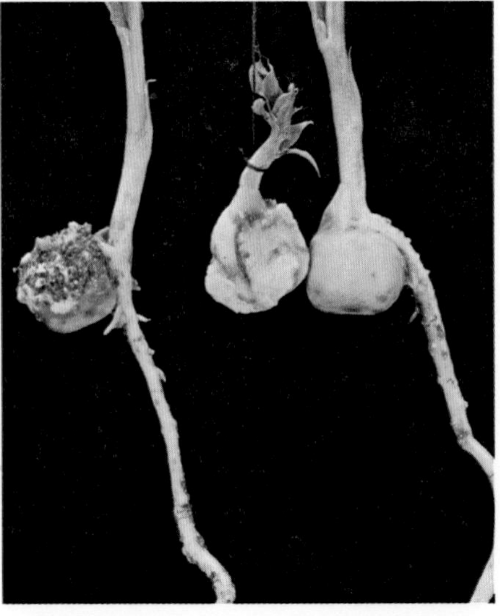

Deficiencies

Plant, like humans, need a balanced diet, and can usually get it from a potting compost. Border soil, however, quite often lacks one or more vital substances – not only nitrates, phosphates, and potash but also elements such as iron, magnesium, and manganese; these elements, although needed in small quantities, are essential to plant health. Magnesium deficiency is readily recognized on tomatoes, for yellow areas develop between the veins of the leaf. Magnesium sulphate (Epsom salts) is a cheap remedy; it is applied to the border soil at the rate of 230 g/m^2 (8 oz/sq yd) and watered in. Potash deficiency often occurs in light, sandy soils, and in severe cases leads to a marked brown edging of plant leaves. High-potash liquid feeds will prevent this recurring.

Insecticides and fungicides

Sprays, dusts, and fumigants (often aerosol-applied) are ways of bringing an active chemical ingredient to bear against pests and disease organisms. Small sprayers of the pump-up type are relatively inexpensive and reliable, and the shaped lance helps to get the spray on to otherwise inaccessible parts of the plant. A nozzle producing fine droplets should be used, and the sprayer

Lighting a greenhouse pyrotechnic fumigant.

must be cleaned thoroughly after use. On no account must a sprayer used in the greenhouse also be used to apply weedkillers.

It is really a matter of preference as to whether one uses sprays or dusts. Some puffer packs make straightforward application easy and accurate, but it is often much more difficult to apply dusts to the underside of leaves.

Fumigants penetrate almost everywhere and consequently are ideal for whole greenhouse treatment—but not, of course, for lean-tos attached to the house. Electrically powered fumigant equipment may be used continuously throughout the year, automatically dispensing minute chemical particles as a vapour; the small built-in heater uses 40 to 60 watts of electricity and a range of chemicals is available. It is wasteful to use such fumigators when the ventilators are open; many gardeners switch them on only during the evening and night.

Pyrotechnic fumigants are available in a range of sizes to suit the volume of the greenhouse. The approximate volume is calculated by multiplying the length by the breadth by the average height. The average height is taken as a point half-way up the roof glazing bars. Such fumigants are best used on warm, still evenings, once you have made sure that the ventilators are tightly closed and any large cracks filled.

Other methods

Enormous advances have been made in plant-breeding techniques in recent years and it is certain that 'breeding in' resistance to pests and diseases will become increasingly effective. A strikingly successful example of this may be seen in the development of the tomato rootstock KNVF, which gives resistance to corky root, root-knot eelworm, verticillium, and fusarium. Tomato varieties resistant to leaf mould, greenback, and tobacco mosaic virus have also been bred and are generally available; so, too, are cucumber varieties offering resistance to powdery and downy mildew.

Biological control is yet another approach. The glasshouse whitefly is effectively controlled by the minute wasp-like parasite *Encarsia formosa*, which inserts its eggs into the fly's nymph stage. The parasites are bred specially for this purpose and are obtainable through the post from a number of propagators. Predators of red spider mite are also available for commercial users, and in the future they may well become available for use by amateur gardeners.

Soil sterilization

If the greenhouse border soil or frame is occupied year after year by the same crops, soil sterilization becomes essential. The ideal sterilant is steam, and steam sterilizers may be available for hire from the larger equipment-hiring shops. Removing the soil from the border, sterilizing it, and then replacing it is, however, a long and laborious process. An alternative method is thoroughly to soak the soil with a 2 per cent solution of formalin. This chemical has the drawback that its fumes kill plants, and consequently the greenhouse has to be completely cleared and left empty for several weeks. Before returning the plants to the greenhouse after this treatment, the soil and atmosphere should be submitted to the 'cress test'. Sprinkle cress seed on to the soil and lightly rake it in. Cress is highly sensitive to the formalin fumes, and only if it grows satisfactorily should plants be returned to the greenhouse.

If the greenhouse is small, it may be worthwhile to change the soil completely, bringing in fresh garden soil. All these methods mentioned are time consuming and the increasing popularity of growing in containers of one type or another reflects their relative ease of use. At all events, the labour and time expended in sterilizing border soils stresses the virtues of rotation.

Annual cleaning

The annual cleaning of the inside and outside of the greenhouse and cold frame is central to good husbandry. The aim is to clear away all rubbish and weeds, kill all lingering pests and diseases, and ensure that the cover, whether of glass or plastic, will once again allow maximum admission of light. It may be done whenever it is most convenient, but the autumn suits many cropping programmes.

INSIDE Remove all plants from the greenhouse as well as any easily moved obstructions such as temporary benching or shelving. Cover with polythene sheeting all electrical points and fixed electric or gas equipment before thoroughly washing the interior with soapy water and a soft brush; the green algal growth that forms on glazing near soil level may require the use of a scrubbing brush. Follow this with a rinse of clear water to which a small quantity of formaldehyde or Jeyes Fluid has been added. Make a note of any repairs that may be necessary. It is advisable to remove sand or shingle from the greenhouse benches. It should be replaced with fresh material if available, or thoroughly washed before it is used again. Both benching and shelving should be well scrubbed before they are returned to the greenhouse.

OUTSIDE Remove weeds growing in the vicinity of the greenhouse and frame, and scrub the panes of glass or polythene cover as well as the framework with soapy water; make sure that the gutters and rainwater butt are cleaned out, too. Algal growth between overlapping panes of glass can often be removed with the aid of a good jet of water from a hosepipe.

Checklist of insecticides and fungicides

The following tables set out most of the important insecticides and fungicides that the greenhouse gardener is likely to use. They are based on information in the *Directory of Garden Chemicals*, 4th edition (London 1979), published by the British Agrochemicals Association.

Most insecticides and fungicides are available in liquid form and are applied by spraying; others are sold as aerosols, powders, granules, or pyrotechnic fumigants. All are quite easy to use, but be careful to follow the manufacturers' instructions as closely as possible.

INSECTICIDES

Active ingredients	**Proprietary brands**	**Applications**
Bacillus thuringiensis	Herbon Thuricide HP (powder)	Control of caterpillars
Bioresmethrin and malathion	Combat Vegetable Insecticide (liquid or aerosol)	Control of fruit and vegetable pests
Borax	Nippon Ant Destroyer (liquid)	Control of ants
Bromophos	Bromophos (powder)	Control of soil pests
Captan and lindane	Murphy Combined Seed Dressing (powder)	Control of pests and diseases of seeds and seedlings
Carbaryl	Boots Garden Insect Powder	Control of caterpillars, etc
	Murphy Sevin Dust	Control of caterpillars, etc
	Murphy Wasp Destroyer (dust)	Control of wasps
Diazinon	Combat Soil Insecticide (granules)	Control of soil pests
	Root Guard (granules)	Control of soil pests
Dichlorvos	Vapona Flykiller (impregnated PVC)	Control of flies in greenhouse
Dicophol/dinocap/ fenitrothion/maneb/ pyrethrum	Murphy Combined Pest and Disease Spray	General insecticide/fungicide
Dimethoate	Boots Systemic Greenfly Killer (liquid)	Control of greenfly and blackfly on flowers and vegetables
	Murphy Systemic Insecticide (liquid)	Control of greenfly, whitefly, red spider, sawfly, scale insects, etc
Fenitrothion	Murphy Fentro (liquid)	Control of greenfly, sawfly, capsids, beetles, caterpillars, etc, on fruit and vegetables
	PBI Fenitrothion (liquid)	
Formothion	Topguard Systemic Liquid	Control of greenfly, blackfly, red spider, caterpillars
	Toprose Systemic Spray	Control of greenfly, red spider, leaf hopper, and small caterpillars on roses
HCH	Murfume BHC Smoke (cone)	Fumigants for control of greenhouse pests
	Fumite BHC Smoke (cone)	
	Boots Ant Destroyer (powder)	Control of ants, woodlice, earwigs, etc
gamma-HCH	Fumite Lindane Smoke (pellets)	Fumigant for control of greenhouse pests
	Murfume Lindane Smoke	Control of greenfly, whitefly, capsids, leaf miner, etc
	Murphy Gamma-BHC Dust	Control of soil pests
	Murphy Lindex Garden Spray	Control of greenfly, earwig, thrips, rootfly, caterpillars, etc
gamma-HCH/malathion	New Kil (spray)	General contact insecticide
gamma-HCH/malathion/ dimethoate	Super Kil (liquid)	Systemic for control of greenhouse pests
gamma-HCH/menazon	Abol-X (liquid)	Systemic for control of greenfly and blackfly
gamma-HCH/pyrethrins/ piperonyl butoxide	Boots Garden Insect Killer (aerosol)	Control of greenfly and blackfly
gamma-HCH/rotenone/ thiram	Hexyl (liquid)	General insecticide/fungicide
gamma-HCH/tecnazene	Fumite Tecnalin Smoke Cone	Fumigant for greenhouse pests
Lindane/malathion	Combat Garden Insecticide Aerosol	Control of greenfly and other pests
Lindane/malathion/ dimethoate	Combat Garden Insecticide (liquid)	Control of greenfly and other pests
Malathion	Boots Greenfly Killer (liquid)	Control of blackfly and greenfly

Active ingredients	Proprietary brands	Applications
Malathion (cont'd)	PBI Malathion Greenfly Killer (liquid)	Control of greenfly, blackfly, whitefly, red spider, thrips, leaf miner, woolly aphids, mealy bugs, and scale insects
	Murphy Greenhouse Aerosol	Control of greenfly, whitefly, red spider, mealy bug, etc
	Murphy Liquid Malathion	Control of greenfly, whitefly, red spider, mealy bug, scale insects, etc
	Murphy Malathion Dust	Control of greenfly, whitefly, thrips, etc
Malathion/dimethoate	Vitax Greenfly/Blackfly Spray (liquid)	Control of greenfly, blackfly, whitefly, red spider, raspberry beetle, leaf miner, thrips, scale insects, and leaf hoppers
Nicotine	XLALL Insecticide (liquid)	Control of aphids
Oxydemeton-methyl	Greenfly Gun (aerosol)	Control of greenfly and blackfly
Pirimicarb	ICI Rapid Greenfly Killer (aerosol or liquid)	Control of greenfly and blackfly
Pirimiphos-methyl	ICI Antkiller (dust)	Control of ants, earwigs, woodlice, and wasps
	Sybol 2 (liquid)	Control of whitefly, red spider, etc
	Sybol 2 (dust)	Control of soil and vegetable pests
Pirimiphos-methyl/ synergised pyrethrins	Sybol 2 (aerosol)	General greenhouse insecticide
	Kerispray (liquid)	General greenhouse insecticide
	Waspend (aerosol)	Control of flying insects
Pyrethrum	Anti-Ant Powder	Control of ants
	Plant Pest Killer (liquid or aerosol)	Control of aphids, etc
Pyrethrum/resmethrin	Bio Sprayday (liquid)	Control of whitefly, greenfly, blackfly, leaf hopper, thrips
Rotenone	Derris – sold in several brands as dust or liquid	General insecticide
Rotenone/sulphur/zineb	Murphy Combined Pest & Disease Dust	General insecticide/fungicide
Trichlorphon	Dipterex (powder)	Control of caterpillars and winged insects
	Tugon (granules)	Control of ants

FUNGICIDES

Active ingredients	Proprietary brands	Applications
Benomyl	Benlate (powder)	General fungicide
Bupirimate/triforine	Nimrod-T (liquid)	Systemic for control of powdery mildew and black spot
Captan	Murphy Orthocide Captan Fungicide (powder)	Control of black spot, *Botrytis*, bulb rot, etc
Captan/lindane	Murphy Combined Seed Dressing (powder)	Control of diseases and pests of seeds and seedlings
Copper compound	Murphy Liquid Copper Fungicide	Control of damping-off in seedlings, leaf mould, blight, mildew, rust, etc
Copper sulphate/ ammonium carbonate	Cheshunt Compound (soluble powder)	Control of damping-off in seedlings
Dicofol/dinocap/ fenitrothion/maneb/ pyrethrum	Murphy Combined Pest and Disease Spray (aerosol)	General fungicide/insecticide
Dinocap	Murphy Dinocap (dust)	Control of powdery mildew
	Murphy Dinocap Mildew Fungicide (powder)	Control of powdery mildew
	Murphy Dinocap Smoke (cone)	Fumigant for control of powdery mildew
	Toprose Mildew Spray	Control of powdery mildew
Oxycarboxin	Plantvax 75 (powder)	Control of rust on flowering plants
Sulphur/zineb/rotenone	Murphy Combined Pest & Disease Dust	General fungicide/insecticide
Tecnazene	Fumite TCNB Smoke Pellets	Fumigant for control of *Botrytis* on tomatoes, etc
	Fumite Fungicide Smoke Cone	Fumigant for control of *Botrytis*, mildew, etc
Thiram	ICI General Garden Fungicide (liquid)	Control of black spot, mildews, rusts, etc
Thiram/gamma-HCH/ rotenone	Hexyl (liquid)	General fungicide/insecticide
Zineb	Dithane (powder)	Control of downy mildew, peach-leaf curl, tomato blight

8 Maintenance

'A STITCH in time saves nine' is a saying that every greenhouse owner should take to heart: on a windy night, a single missing pane of glass can very easily have multiplied to nine by the morning. The annual maintenance of greenhouses, frames, and equipment need not be a major task and is perhaps best carried out at the time of the annual cleaning. It is convenient to consider greenhouses and garden frames together, although the latter are unlikely to cause many problems.

The structure

Painted wooden greenhouse frames will need exterior painting every four to five years and interior painting every five to six years. An exterior-grade white paint of good quality should be used. An undercoat as well as a topcoat will be required; if the old coats are stripped down to the wood, knots must be treated with knotting and a primer will need to be applied before the undercoat. The wood must be perfectly dry when paint is applied, and on the glazing bars the paint should lap 3 mm ($\frac{1}{8}$ in) on to the panes to seal the gap between wood and glass.

With greenhouses of western red cedar, treat the timber internally and externally every two to three years with preservatives sold specially for the purpose: all that is needed is a light rubbing down with a fine grade of sandpaper and a single application of the preservative.

Greenhouses that have a framework of steel are normally galvanized. However, this surface treatment may be removed locally if knocked, and rust will quickly develop at the point of damage. Remove all rust with emery cloth or a wire brush, and paint the affected areas with a metal primer and then with a finishing coat. It is useless to paint over rusted steel.

Greenhouse ventilators should at all times fit snugly when closed, so attend to individual ventilators as and when trouble arises. Some designs of hinge require annual application of a lubricant, and if automatic vent gear is fitted the manufacturer's recommendations regarding maintenance should be followed – a few drops of oil on the pivots may be all that is necessary. Ensure that doors, too, are draughtproof; if necessary fit draught excluders.

Replace cracked and broken glass with panes of similar thickness – take a bit of the old glass with you when ordering if you are uncertain as to thickness. Some putty-less glazing systems make glass changing easy. If glass is available and simply requires cutting to size the modern wheeled glass cutters make the task relatively easy; the carborundum wheel should be lightly oiled before use. Several thicknesses of newspaper spread on a perfectly flat surface make the ideal cutting bed and sufficient pressure should be applied when cutting to score the glass along its entire length but not to cut through it. Tapping the underside of the cut with the glasscutter will complete the job by causing the glass to break neatly along the line.

In wooden greenhouses and frames replace any rotting timbers with wood that has been pressure-treated with preservative (not creosote). If the trouble is rectified at an early stage the whole piece may not need changing; a skilled woodworker may be able to splice in a suitable length, thus saving both time and money.

Water dripping within the greenhouse is not merely annoying; it may be harmful to plants. Dripping may arise through excessive condensation, owing to incorrect ventilation; or it may be due to a leaky roof. In the latter case the source should be treated if possible; this is not always easy, for water often runs down a glazing bar before dripping. The troublesome area can often be dealt with by use of a waterproof adhesive tape, or by mastic putty applied straight from the tube.

Once a year check the greenhouse foundation plates and resite any that may have shifted. It is essential that they fit well, for uneven foundations are not only a common cause of draughts but may eventually lead to frame stress and broken glass. Polythene-clad greenhouses usually require re-covering every two years, and this restores a good-as-new appearance.

The annual spring-clean of the greenhouse involves cleaning it thoroughly inside and out. Spring may not in fact be the most convenient time, and many gardeners do this job in the autumn. Make sure that all algal growth is removed from the glass. Western red cedar structures (as here) must be treated inside and out with a special preservative every two or three years.

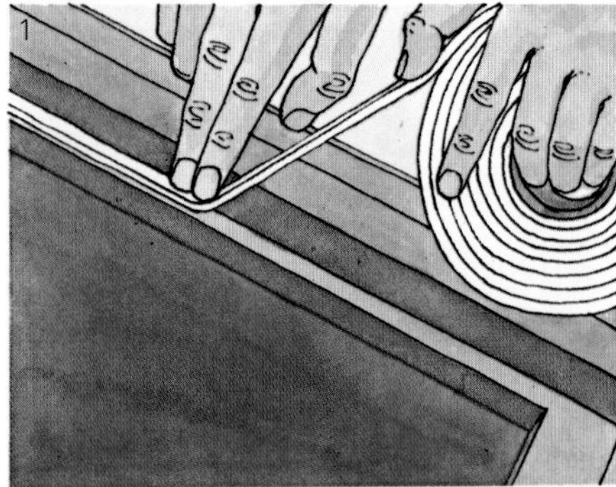

Use of self-adhesive bedding tape instead of putty speeds re-glazing. 1 Tape is applied to glazing bar; 2 Glass is fitted, then secured with glazing sprigs; 3 Glass is sealed on outer surface with more tape.

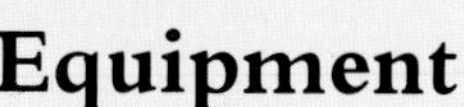

Equipment

Most greenhouse equipment on the market today is robust and will give many years of satisfactory service provided it receives a little attention annually. Electrical gadgets abound and their reliability is rarely questioned – and for this reason their maintenance is often neglected. Electrical fan heaters circulate large volumes of air and in certain conditions can get very dirty inside. Dust within the casing should be removed from time to time, and the fan bearings lubricated with a light oil.

A faulty thermostat can quickly lead to very heavy fuel bills in cold weather, and in the case of electric heating a meter within the greenhouse, read and recorded weekly, will provide both a check and a guide to running costs. Thermostats need checking annually and should be recalibrated every two years. To do this it is necessary to compare them at a range of temperatures with a thermometer known to be accurate. Many thermostats click quite loudly when switching on and switching off and have a tolerance of 1 to 2°C. Check also the bearings of the small fans fitted in some aspirated screens; they, too, need occasional oiling. Greenhouse lighting, if of the fluorescent kind, attracts dust and the tubes should be regularly wiped over with a slightly moist, soapy cloth, especially if they are providing supplementary lighting for purposes of cultivation. It is as well to check visually all internal electric wiring, for rodents occasionally play havoc with the insulation; at the same time check that the earthing wire is securely fastened to its earthing point.

The efficiency of mist propagation equipment depends to a large extent on the efficiency of the sensing mechanism. The artificial 'leaf' found on older equipment needs cleaning regularly, and this is best done by inverting it in dilute hydrochloric acid for a few minutes, afterwards rinsing it in clean water. The mist-spray nozzles need thorough cleaning periodically and this should be done before a busy propagating period. If watering is by capillary benching, replace the mats annually.

Where heating is by hot-water pipes, ensure these are kept painted – a matt black heat-resisting paint is best. Avoid metallic-based paints such as aluminium, because they reduce heat output; never use bitumastic paints because the fumes they give off when the pipes are hot are harmful to plants. Electric tubular heaters are also prone to rust and should be repainted when necessary.

As in the home, in the greenhouse there is a large number of things that *can* go wrong and some of them are expensive to replace. The best way to prevent this happening is to establish a system of regular inspection and maintenance, so that potential sources of trouble are detected early.

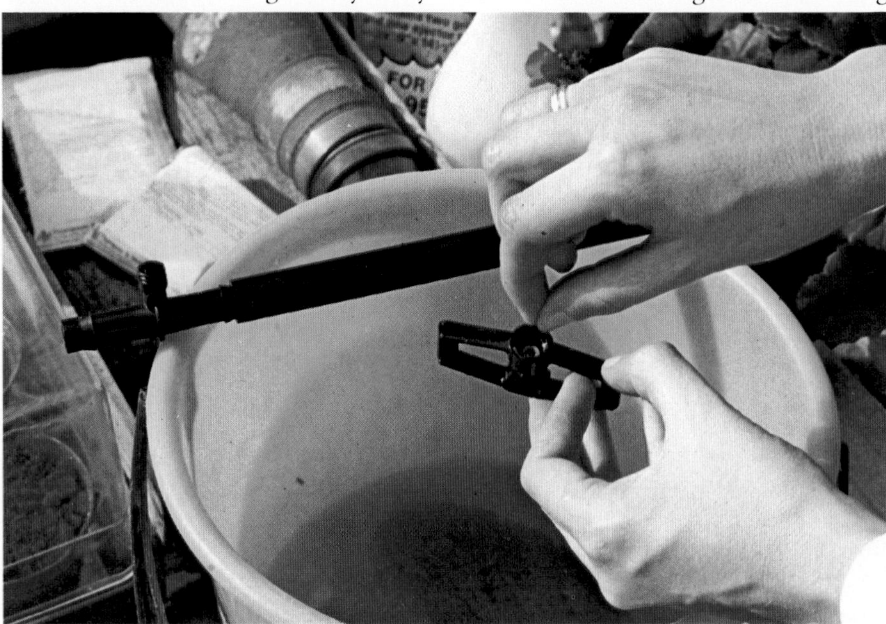

Left Mist propagating units should be partly dismantled and cleaned; the spray nozzles, especially, may become partially blocked unless they are cleaned periodically. **Right** When summer crops are over, the benching should be re-installed for winter pot-plant displays and spring propagation.

9 A Calendar of Greenhouse Work

January

As the Christmas-flowering chrysanthemums finish flowering cut them back hard and box up those stools from which cuttings will be taken later. Bring in rhubarb for forcing and plant the crowns under benching if space is available. In soil-warmed borders and frames sow 'Forcing French Breakfast' radishes, 'Amsterdam Forcing' carrots, and 'May Queen' lettuces.

In the south of England it is time to start the propagating season. Take cuttings of the autumn-flowering chrysanthemums and sow seed of F_1 hybrid geraniums and the fibrous-rooted begonias. From now through to March sow antirrhinums and garden annuals required for greenhouse display. Watch out for slugs and snails – it is better to put out a little bait from time to time than to lose a pan of special seedlings overnight. If greenhouse borders are uncropped, prepare them, and find out whether the soil is acid or alkaline by using the *p*H testing solution.

February

This is quite early enough in the north of England to begin many of the activities listed above. Start dahlia tubers into growth by boxing them up in damp peat or old cucumber compost; cutting material will then be available from March onwards. Prune vines, cutting back the lateral growths to two eyes. House strawberry plants for fruiting in May.

Make a further small sowing of radish, broadcasting the seed rather than sowing it in drills. Sow peas in boxes for planting outside later. Propagate hydrangeas by cuttings taken from selected plants. Sow seeds of *Passiflora* (passion flower) and lightly prune established *Passiflora* plants; make a sowing of *Solanum* (Christmas cherry). February is usually a convenient month to erect temporary benching and fit shelving for young plants.

March

Owners of unheated greenhouses or propagating equipment will not have been able to do much in the way of plant raising to date, but from now on they will have to use every bit of space. The emphasis this month should be on seed and plant propagation. Sow tomatoes for cool and cold greenhouse growing; also cucumbers, courgettes, and sweet peppers. Make further sowings of radish and, where emphasis is on early vegetable production, sow beetroot, carrots, and turnips. From March through to June sow freesias. Plant out tomatoes in a warm greenhouse if the soil or compost temperature is at least 13°C (57°F).

April

Asparagus ferns grow rapidly and need dividing every year or so; now is a good time to do this. Orders placed for perpetual-flowering carnations are often delivered this month; pot them

Above left Start dahlia tubers in damp peat in February. Cuttings are ready in about a month. **Right** The limited space in a small greenhouse may be overstretched at some times of the year, so plan cropping in advance.

up immediately they arrive. If a mist-propagating unit is available, two or three days under mist will speed up their establishment. This is the month to make up hanging baskets for the greenhouse or home.

Overwintered lettuce should be ready for cutting; when the majority have been cut, clear away the debris and make ready for the following crop without delay, Sow melons. Start runner beans for planting outdoors next month. If a few glasshouse climbers are required, make a sowing of *Pharbitis tricolor* (morning glory) in a pan. Prevent damping-off of seedlings by watering regularly with Cheshunt compound. Tie in the vines.

May

Many plants will be moved this month from the shelter and warmth of the greenhouse to the frames in which they will be hardened off. Pot-grown camellias and newly-potted mid-season and late decorative chrysanthemums should be moved to their summer quarters outside. Pot-grown roses should by now have developed spring flowers and may be moved to plunge beds outdoors. This entails digging out an area to the same depth as the pots and spacing the pots in it so that each plant has ample room to grow. Fill the area between the pots with ashes, coarse sand, or peat, and keep this moist. The pot tops may be covered by a thin layer of topsoil. Plants are individually watered in the normal manner, but water loss from the pots is reduced and the root system kept cool.

Solanum should be moved to a cold frame for the summer months. Sow *Primula kewensis, P. obconica,* and ornamental capsicums. Remove the side shoots of tomatoes at an early stage. The training of cucumber plants is likely to occupy much of your time this month.

June

After the hectic spring activities, June may offer something of a respite. Watch out for scorch arising from very hot sunshine; many mixed collections of pot-grown decorative plants may need to be shaded. Blinds are ideal; alternatively, use a shading compound on some of the glass to shade those plants that require it.

Plunge hydrangeas in their summer quarters outdoors. Sow calceolarias (and cinerarias if earlier sowings have not been made). Move young cycla-

Making up a hanging basket: 1 Line half way up sides with sphagnum moss; 2 Add layer of fibrous loam; 3 Half fill basket with compost, then water well; 4 Insert plants through side of basket; 5 Add more loam, compost, and additional plants to centre; 6 Completed basket; feed and water regularly.

men plants raised from seed to shaded frames. Start thinning the bunches of grapes on the vines, using vine scissors; this will need to be done several times at two to three-week intervals. The aim is to finish up with bunches of well-spaced large grapes. Dismantle shelving to allow maximum light to reach the developing plants beneath it.

July

Start cyclamen corms into growth if this method is being used. Take the first batch of pelargonium cuttings, which should root easily at this time of year. Sow *Primula malacoides* for winter flowering. Vegetable harvesting should be in full swing in polythene and plastic greenhouses, and second sowings may be made following crop clearance; remember to give the plot additional fertilizer as a base dressing.

Pests and diseases are especially rife in mid-summer, and you should intensify your routine examinations of plants at this time of year, including those in frames and plunge beds.

August

The holiday month. It is risky to leave the greenhouse unattended even for a few days. Try to come to some arrangement with a neighbouring greenhouse owner for it to be looked after in your absence, offering to help him in return.

Sow winter lettuce seed; when the seedlings are large enough, prick them out into soil blocks or peat pots. Maiden strawberry plants for spring forcing should be received this month from specialist growers. (Politely refuse young strawberry plants offered by friendly neighbours: they are very likely to be contaminated with one of the strawberry viruses). Take a second batch of pelargonium cuttings. Plant freesia corms. Prepare lifted chrysanthemums for their move to greenhouse borders next month.

September

With the time of autumn frosts approaching, the greenhouse must be prepared to house plants that have spent the summer out of doors. Tomatoes and cucumbers that are still carrying fruits may have to be sacrificed to make way for mid-season and late-flowering chrysanthemums. Transfer calceolarias from the frame to the heated greenhouse and, late in the month, rehouse the *Solanum* and one-year-old cyclamen plants. This is also the time to sow cyclamen seed for winter flowering 15 months hence. Plant out overwintering lettuce in unheated structures and frames; put down slug bait.

October

Move camellias and hydrangeas back into the protection of the cool greenhouse. Box up stools of selected outdoor chrysanthemums as they finish flowering to provide cuttings in the new year; it is advisable to wash all garden soil off their roots before boxing them – any slug eggs will get washed away at the same time. Sift potting compost between the roots and lightly water in.

November

Roses ordered for greenhouse growing should be received this month; pot them directly into 200 mm (8 in) pots but do not bring them into the greenhouse until late December. Sow tomato seed in heat if the earliest fruits are required. Box up the mid-season and late-flowering chrysanthemums.

Check for draughts at doors and ventilators, and if necessary fit draught-excluders to retain heat. Clear 150-gauge polythene sheeting fixed along the sides of the greenhouse will reduce draughts and conserve heat; do not take it completely up the ridge bars as it will cut out too much light and may cause humidity problems.

Border soil-warming cables are useful for winter cropping. Lay the cables on a bed of sand and place a length of chicken netting over them before replacing border topsoil.

December

There should be lettuce to cut in soil-warmed borders and frames, and young lettuce plants planted now in these borders will be ready for March cutting. Check on the accuracy of the heating thermostats. Wash all used plant pots and seed trays in formalin (remember to do this outside the greenhouse, as the fumes will kill plants). Order seeds and plants such as chrysanthemums, carnations, and orchids from your nursery man.

Index

Acknowledgments

The publishers would like to thank the following organizations and individuals for their kind permission to reproduce the photographs in this book:

A-Z Botanical Collection Limited 41, 48, 53 centre; Bernard Alfieri 19, 23, 72, 75; Amdega Limited 7; Rodney Bond (Adespoton Film Services) 12; Pat Brindley 14, 27 below right, 39, 42, 44, 46, 47, 52, 55, 57 below right, 82 below left; Bruce Coleman Limited 40, 49; Eric Crichton 33; Michael Crockett 8, 25 below right, 26, 30, 35, 54, 64 above and below right and below left, 65, 66 above and below right, 71, 74, 87, 88, 89, 90; Edenlite Limited 1, 16 above left, 29, 93; Mary Evans Picture Library 6; Brian Furner 9, 32, 67; Garden Relax 16 below left; John Harris 20, 21, 34, 51, 60 above and below right, 62, 66 below right, 83 below right, 85; George Hyde 82 below right; I.C.I. Limited (Plant Protection Division) 84; M.A. Knight 24 below left; London Brick Buildings Limited 2, 38; Marley Greenhouses 17, 25 above right; Natural History Photographic Agency 15 left; David Prout 15 below right, 81; Roberts Electrical Company Limited 27 below left and centre and above right, 28 below; Malcolm Robertson 56, 69; Thomas Rochford and Sons Limited 28 above; Royal Horticultural Society's Garden, Wisley 83 above centre; Harry Smith Horticultural Photographic Collection 5, 36, 53 above right, 57 above right, 63, 73, 77, 79, 83 above left; Spectrum Colour Library 45, 91; Pamla Toler 10; Michael Warren 24 above left, 59, 61, 68, 70.

Drawings by David Bryant.